PHARMACOLOGY - RESEARCH, SAFETY TESTING AND REGULATION

PHARMACEUTICAL INDUSTRY DEVELOPMENTS

SPECIALTY DRUGS, COUPONS, REVERSE PAYMENTS AND PRODUCT HOPPING

PHARMACOLOGY - RESEARCH, SAFETY TESTING AND REGULATION

Additional books in this series can be found on Nova's website under the Series tab.

Additional e-books in this series can be found on Nova's website under the e-book tab.

PHARMACOLOGY - RESEARCH, SAFETY TESTING AND REGULATION

PHARMACEUTICAL INDUSTRY DEVELOPMENTS

SPECIALTY DRUGS, COUPONS, REVERSE PAYMENTS AND PRODUCT HOPPING

KRISTY BISHOP
EDITOR

nova publishers
New York

Library of Congress Cataloging-in-Publication Data

ISBN: 978-1-63484-649-3

Published by Nova Science Publishers, Inc. † New York

CONTENTS

PREFACE

Specialty drugs are one of the fastest-growing areas of health care spending. There is no one set definition of specialty drugs, although insurers and other health care payers often characterize them as prescription products requiring extra handling or administration that are used to treat complex diseases including hepatitis C, multiple sclerosis, and cancer. High cost can trigger a specialty drug designation. Biologics, or drugs derived from living cells, are often but not always deemed to be specialty drugs. This book provides background on specialty drugs. To put specialty drug development, distribution, and spending in context, the book provides information about broader U.S. prescription drug pricing, insurance, and regulatory trends. Furthermore, this book explains the difference between coupons and other pharmaceutical assistance and incentive programs offered by manufacturers, pharmacies, states, and nonprofit organizations; outlines federal laws and regulations and private-sector policies relating to coupons and other financial incentives for consumers/patients to purchase prescription drugs; and introduces and analyzes innovation and competition policy issues associated with the pharmaceutical industry.

In: Pharmaceutical Industry Developments ISBN: 978-1-63484-649-3
Editor: Kristy Bishop

Chapter 1

SPECIALTY DRUGS: BACKGROUND AND POLICY CONCERNS*

Suzanne M. Kirchhoff

SUMMARY

Specialty drugs are one of the fastest-growing areas of health care spending. There is no one set definition of specialty drugs, although insurers and other health care payers often characterize them as prescription products requiring extra handling or administration that are used to treat complex diseases including hepatitis C, multiple sclerosis, and cancer. High cost can trigger a specialty drug designation. Biologics, or drugs derived from living cells, are often but not always deemed to be specialty drugs.

Over the past several years, spending for specialty drugs has been growing at a faster rate than spending for other pharmaceuticals. For example, in 2014, U.S. prescription drug spending rose by 13% from the previous year—the fastest pace since 2001—led by a 26.5% increase in spending for specialty drugs (with much of that spending for drugs to treat hepatitis C), according to industry and government data. Specialty medications now account for about one-third of total U.S. prescription drug spending, and some analysts predict they could make up as much as one-half of total drug spending by 2018.

* This is an edited, reformatted and augmented version of a Congressional Research Service publication, No. R44132, dated August 3, 2015.

Insurers have tried to control spending for specialty drugs, in part, by increasing cost sharing for beneficiaries of their health care plans and taking other steps to limit access under their policies. Consumer advocates say that these efforts have undercut some of the recent gains in prescription drug insurance coverage. During the past decade, Congress has expanded consumer access to prescription drugs by enacting the Medicare Part D prescription drug program, requiring certain health plans to provide prescription drug benefits as part of the Patient Protection and Affordable Care Act (ACA; P.L. 111-148, as amended), and expanding the state-federal Medicaid program. Some lawmakers now are focused on ensuring that private and public health care payers do not structure insurance benefits in such a way that certain enrollees cannot afford to fill prescriptions for high-cost medications. During the 113th Congress, for example, lawmakers introduced legislation to cap out-of-pocket spending by insured consumers for specialty drugs. In recent years, states such as New York and Delaware have enacted laws that limit consumer cost sharing for prescription drugs. Dozens of states also have passed laws that bar insurers from imposing higher out-of-pocket charges for oral specialty cancer drugs than for traditional treatments. Others have debated bills to require insurers to detail drug development costs..

Although some of the legislative proposals can reduce consumer out-of-pocket costs, they do not address the overall price of specialty drugs. Congress historically has attempted to improve prescription drug affordability by providing incentives to increase supply and market competition. Lawmakers fund basic drug research through the National Institutes of Health and provide nonrefundable tax credits for qualified research spending. Federal laws including the Orphan Drug Act of 1982 (P.L. 97-414), the Drug Price Competition and Patent Term Restoration Act of 1984 (Hatch-Waxman; P.L. 98-417), and the ACA provide financial incentives for both new, breakthrough drugs and lower-cost substitutes. Those incentives may provide some financial relief in the longer term, but in the short run federal programs and private payers face high upfront prices and spending for new specialty therapies, such as recently introduced treatments for hepatitis C and cancer.

This report provides background on specialty drugs. To put specialty drug development, distribution, and spending in context, the report provides information about broader U.S. prescription drug pricing, insurance, and regulatory trends.

INTRODUCTION

Specialty drugs are one of the fastest-growing areas of health care spending.[1] Although there is no commonly accepted definition of specialty drugs, insurers and other health care payers generally characterize them as expensive prescription products requiring extra handling or administration (such as injection or infusion) that are used to treat complex diseases including multiple sclerosis, cancer, and hepatitis C. Biologics—complex drugs derived from living organisms[2]—are often but not always specialty drugs, as are so-called orphan drugs, which are targeted at rare diseases or disorders.[3]

U.S. spending for specialty drugs increased by 26.5% in 2014 as new drugs for treating hepatitis C came to the market, according to a broad analysis of pharmaceutical market data.[4] Other, more targeted studies also show rapid growth for specialty products.[5] According to one of the largest U.S. pharmacy benefit managers (PBMs),[6] specialty drugs account for less than 1% of U.S. prescriptions but about one-third of prescription drug spending. [7] Some health care industry analysts and PBMs predict that specialty drugs could account for half of all annual prescription drug spending before the end of the decade.[8] To date, the rapid increases in specialty spending have been driven mainly by price inflation, although utilization is starting to play a larger role as manufacturers bring a wider array of specialty drugs to market, including products with broad applications, such as the treatments for hepatitis C.[9]

What Is a Pharmacy Benefit Manager?

Pharmacy benefit managers (PBMs) serve as intermediaries between drug manufacturers and health care payers, such as self-insured businesses; insurance companies, including insurers that participate in Medicaid and Medicare; and union-run health plans. PBMs handle prescription billing; negotiate drug prices with drug companies; and create retail pharmacy networks for insurers, including contracting with mail-order pharmacies and negotiating reimbursement rates with them. PBMs also design insurance formularies, which are lists of drugs covered by an insurance plan.

PBMs oversee prescription drug benefits for more than 210 million Americans. The largest PBMs include Express Scripts, with 28% market share; CVS Caremark, with 27% market share; UnitedHealth Group, with 10% market share; and Catamaran, with 7% market share.[10] Other large

PBMs include Prime Therapeutics, MedImpact, and Cigna.[11]

Consolidation in the PBM industry is ongoing. Drug retailers have merged with PBMs to provide integrated health services. CVS Health is a retail pharmacy chain and a PBM. The Rite Aid drug store chain in 2015 purchased the PBM EnvisionRx.[12] Some insurers operate their own PBMs, such as a group of Blue Cross and Blue Shield plans that owns Prime Therapeutics, and UnitedHealthcare, which owns OptumRx. (Catamaran and OptumRx combined in 2015.)[13]

The growing use of specialty drugs poses complex issues for private insurers and government health programs such as Medicare, Medicaid, and the Veterans Health Administration.[14] Specialty drugs can provide marked improvement or a cure for individuals with serious diseases, thereby reducing the need for hospitalizations and other health services. The potential long-term benefits of specialty drugs may not always offset their higher up-front costs, however. In addition, because the U.S. health care system is decentralized and consumers may change insurance providers, one insurer may bear the cost of the drugs while another insurer may reap the benefit of reduced health care spending for an enrollee treated with specialty pharmaceuticals.[15]

Insurers and employers, and the PBMs with which they contract, control drug costs in part by negotiating discounts and rebates with manufacturers. Because there are no ready substitutes for many newly introduced specialty drugs, health payers may have less ability to negotiate significant price reductions. To contain spending, many health care payers also control enrollees' access to specialty drugs under their plans. Insurers may require enrollees to obtain prior authorization for specialty prescriptions (meaning the insurer must review and approve the prescription before paying for it), impose higher cost sharing for the drugs (charge higher out-of-pocket amounts to fill a prescription), or cover the drugs for only the sickest patients. The net result is uneven access to the products for consumers in private insurance plans and some government programs, in terms of both availability and cost.[16]

Congress, which plays a major role in the prescription drug market, has attempted to address broad issues regarding prescription drug price and availability by expanding insurance coverage and providing incentives for pharmaceutical manufacturers to increase the supply of drugs. In the past decade, Congress has provided subsidized drug coverage to tens of millions of consumers by implementing the Medicare Prescription Drug, Improvement, and Modernization Act of 2003 (MMA; P.L. 108-173), which created the Medicare Part D prescription drug program[17] and the Patient Protection and

Affordable Care Act (ACA; P.L. 111-148, as amended), which requires insurers to provide basic prescription drug benefits in qualified-individual and small-group health plans sold on exchanges. In addition, as part of the ACA, Congress expanded Medicaid,[18] which also provides prescription drug benefits. Reflecting the increasing government role, the federal share of U.S. prescription drug spending rose to a projected 41% in 2014 from 25% in 2005—the year before Medicare Part D took full effect. [19]

Lawmakers also have provided patent protection and other financial incentives for pharmaceutical manufacturers to develop drugs through the Orphan Drug Act of 1982 (P.L. 97 414); the Drug Price Competition and Patent Term Restoration Act of 1984 (Hatch-Waxman; P.L. 98-417);[20] and the ACA.[21] Lawmakers fund basic research through the National Institutes of Health[22] and provide nonrefundable tax credits to the industry for qualified research spending.[23]

Common Insurance Terms Used in This Report

Co-payment: A fixed dollar amount that an enrollee in a health care plan pays for a product or service covered by the plan. For example, an insurer may charge a $20 co-payment for a physician visit or a $5 co-payment for a prescription drug.

Coinsurance: The percentage share that an enrollee in a health insurance plan pays for a product or service covered by the plan. An insurer may charge 10% coinsurance for a $100 prescription drug, meaning the consumer's out-of-pocket cost is $10.

Deductible: The amount an enrollee is required to pay for health care services or products before his or her insurance plan begins to provide coverage. An enrollee in an insurance plan with a $500 deductible would be responsible for paying for the first $500 in health care services. In some insurance plans, the deductible does not apply to certain services, such as preventive care. Insurance plans vary regarding whether beneficiaries must meet a deductible for prescription drug coverage.

Formulary: A list of prescription drugs covered by an insurance plan. In an effort to control costs, insurers are imposing what are known as *tight formularies* that include a more limited number of drugs. Insurers also are using *tiered formularies*, under which patients are charged lower co-payments or coinsurance for less expensive generic drugs and certain brand-name drugs[24] that are designated by the plan as preferred drugs because they are lower cost or deemed by an insurer to be safer or more effective. Under these tiered formularies, patients are charged higher co-payments or coinsurance for more expensive drugs or drugs that the plan deems to be less effective.

Out-of-Pocket Costs: The total amount an insured consumer pays each year for covered health care services that are not reimbursed by an insurance plan. Out-of-pocket costs can include deductibles, co-payments, and coinsurance.

Out-of-Pocket Maximum: The maximum amount an enrollee must pay before his or her health insurance plan covers 100% of health benefits. Certain costs, such as premiums, generally are not counted toward an out-of-pocket cap.

Pharmacy Network: A group of retail, mail-order, and specialty pharmacies that contract with health insurers to dispense covered drugs at a set price. Network pharmacies also may provide other services under contract, such as monitoring patient adherence to drugs. Some states require insurance companies to contract with any willing pharmacy that agrees to meet their financial terms. In other states, insurers may contract with a smaller network of preferred pharmacies. Insurers say they have more ability to negotiate price concessions in preferred networks.

Premium: The amount an enrollee pays for health insurance coverage. Many plans charge monthly premiums, but premiums also can be assessed on a quarterly or annual basis.

Sources: Information from Congressional Research Service (CRS) reports, Healthcare.gov, and other sources.

Recently, there has been an increased focus on specialty drugs. During the 114th Congress, lawmakers introduced bills to cap insured consumers' out-of-pocket spending for high-priced drugs.[25] Some state governments have enacted laws to limit consumer out-of-pocket spending for specialty drugs,[26] and many have prohibited insurers from charging consumers higher cost sharing for certain newer specialty cancer drugs than for existing treatments.[27] In addition, some ACA state health insurance exchanges have moved to limit prescription drug cost sharing in exchange-offered insurance plans.[28] This report provides information about the specialty drug market and insurance coverage. To put specialty drug development, distribution, and spending in context, the report also provides information about broader U.S. prescription drug pricing, insurance, and regulatory trends.

U.S. PRESCRIPTION DRUG MARKET

The United States is the world's largest pharmaceutical market, making up more than one-third of total global drug spending.[29] Roughly 10 cents of every U.S. health care dollar is spent on prescription drugs ($305 billion in 2014).[30]

According to federal data, from 1980 through 2007, U.S. prescription drug spending rose by about 11% annually, on average.[31] From 2008 through 2013, the pace of annual drug spending slowed to about 2% on average.[32] (See Figure 1 for annual growth rates.) There were several reasons for the recent slowdown, including the 2007 economic recession, which also helped reduce overall U.S. health care costs;[33] the increasing use of insurer drug-utilization controls; and the introduction of fewer blockbuster, brand-name drugs than in previous years. Rising utilization of lower-cost generic drugs was a major factor in holding down costs, as patents for a number of best-selling brand name drugs expired.[34]

Hatch-Waxman Act

In 1984, Congress enacted the Hatch-Waxman Act to spur the development of lower-cost generic drugs. Generic drugs are identical to traditional brand-name drugs in dosage, safety, strength, route of administration, quality, performance characteristics, and intended use.[35] The act provided manufacturers of innovative prescription drugs with patent protection and a period of marketing exclusivity; created a generic drug approval process to help companies bring products to the market more quickly once the patent for an original brand-name drug expired; and established procedures for resolving patent disputes arising from applications to market generic drugs.[36] Consumers and health care payers can realize significant savings from generic drugs, which can cost 75%-80% less than an original brand-name drug.[37] The average price of a brand-name drug also may decline after a generic comes to the market. Only 19% of prescriptions were filled with generics when Hatch-Waxman was enacted. The generic market share rose to 86% in 2013 and accounted for 28% of U.S. drug spending.

In its latest forecast for national health spending, the Centers for Medicare & Medicaid Services (CMS) projected that U.S. prescription drug spending rose by 12.6% in 2014, due in part to increased specialty drug use, and would average 6.3% annual growth from 2015 through 2024.[38] (See Figure 1.) CMS says ACA implementation is helping drive the higher spending, as millions of Americans become newly insured or obtain more comprehensive coverage, including prescription drug benefits.[39] The improving economy and improved drug adherence are other noted factors, along with the fact that Americans are using more prescription drugs for longer periods of time to treat chronic ailments such as diabetes or heart disease.

Some analysts predict that generic drug utilization will level off at about 91%-92% of filled prescriptions in the next several years, meaning generic substitution could play a smaller role in limiting drug spending.[40] In addition to the fact that fewer blockbuster, traditional drugs will lose patent protection than has been the case during the past several years, a greater share of drugs under development are biologics for which there are not many lower-cost substitutes. Manufacturers also have increased prices for a number of existing brand-name and generic drugs.[41]

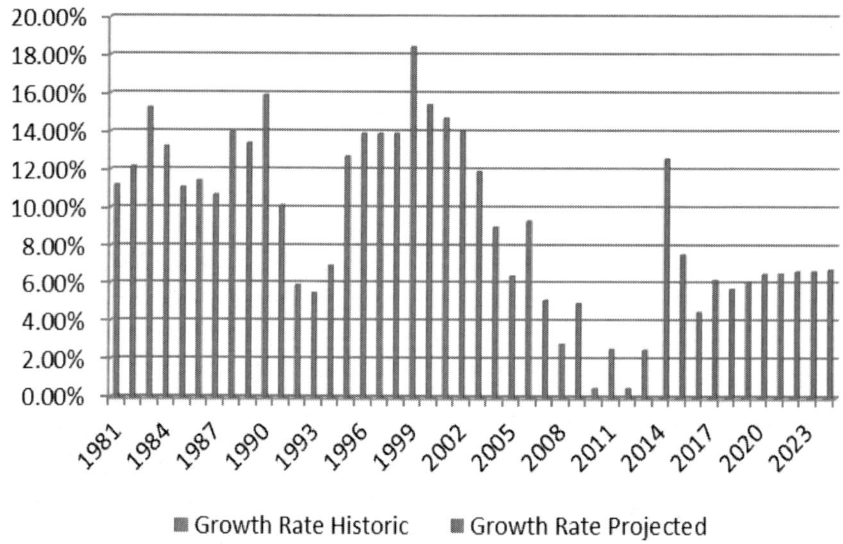

Sources: Centers for Medicare & Medicaid Services (CMS), *National Health Expenditure Projections, 2014-2024*, Table 11, and CMS Historical Data.

Figure 1. U.S. Prescription Drug Spending 1980-2024 (annual percentage change from previous year).

SPECIALTY DRUGS

As previously noted, specialty drugs are broadly described as prescription drugs that are expensive; need special handling or administration, such as drugs that are infused or injected; have limited distribution; are targeted at a narrow group of chronic diseases; or are biologics.[42] (See Figure 2.) Even those general categorizations do not hold across all insurers and government health care programs. In the voluntary Medicare Part D program, for example, price is the main factor used to determine whether an insurer may classify a drug as a specialty product and impose higher cost sharing.[43]

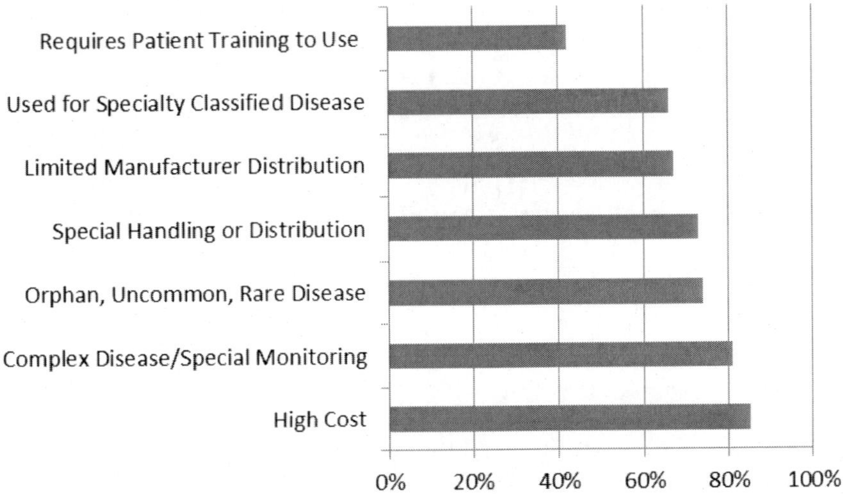

Source: EMD Serono *Specialty Digest,* 10th Edition, p. 10.

Notes: Data are based on a survey of 91 Medicare Advantage and commercial managed care health plans representing 124 million covered lives. For those plans that cited high cost as a factor, 86% defined high cost as more than $600 per month.

Figure 2. Factors Determining Specialty Drug Designation (leading criteria for specialty drug determination cited by managed care plans).

Biologics

Many specialty drugs are biologics. Biologics are products derived from a living organism that can be many times the size of a conventional (small-molecule) drug and have a more complex structure. Biologics may be sensitive to heat and contamination, making them more difficult to ship and store. Biologics often must be injected, although a growing number are available in oral form. Examples of biologics include monoclonal antibodies for treating cancer,[44] botox, and shingles and flu vaccines.[45] Pharmaceutical firms are focusing on development of biologic drugs, which accounted for about 22% of sales by the world's top pharmaceutical companies in 2013, according to research.[46]

Congress has provided 12 years of product exclusivity for certain biologic drugs,[47] which limits manufacturers' initial market competition and increases their pricing power. Lawmakers also have attempted to spur development of lower-cost *biosimilar* products, similar to earlier efforts to stimulate development of generic products. Congress enacted the Biologics Price Competition and Innovation Act of 2009 (BPCIA) as Title VII of the ACA.[48] The ACA/BPCIA gives the U.S. Food and Drug Administration (FDA) authority to license products shown to be biosimilar to or interchangeable with an FDA-licensed biological product.[49] The Congressional Budget Office (CBO) has estimated that the ACA/BPCIA eventually could reduce insurer and consumer spending for biologics.[50]

Orphan Drugs

Many orphan drugs (which often are biologics) are classified as specialty drugs by insurers and other payers. An orphan drug is a drug targeted at a rare disease or condition (1) affecting fewer than 200,000 persons in the United States or (2) affecting more than 200,000 persons in the United States but for which there is no reasonable expectation that the sales of the drug will be sufficient to offset the costs.[51] The Orphan Drug Act of 1982 (P.L. 97-142) provides seven years of marketing exclusivity, tax credits, and FDA assistance with the review process as incentives for pharmaceutical firms to develop such drugs.[52]

Of the 41 novel new drugs approved by the FDA in calendar year 2014, 41% were orphan drugs, the highest annual total since passage of the Orphan Drug Act.[53]

Manufacturers often set high prices for orphan drugs.[54] Pharmaceutical companies point out that they have a narrow patient population from which to recoup development and marketing costs. Some orphan drugs expand beyond their target market if they are effective for treating other conditions that were not part of the original FDA approval process (a situation known as off-label use).[55] Some orphan drugs have reached blockbuster status, meaning they have sales of more than $1 billion per year.[56]

SPECIALTY DRUG SPENDING TRENDS

Specialty medications grew from 23% of total U.S. prescription drug spending in 2010 to 33% in 2014 and accounted for about 73% of overall drug spending growth during that period, according to one analysis.[57] PBM data show that specialty drug spending has been growing much faster than spending on traditional drugs. For example, businesses and commercial insurers served by PBM Express Scripts posted a 30.9% increase in specialty drug spending in 2014, compared with a 6.4% rise for traditional drugs.[58]

Price inflation has been the main driver of specialty drug spending in recent years, but volume growth played a larger role in 2014 because 161,000 people began treatment with hepatitis C drugs. According to IMS Health, spending for hepatitis C drugs amounted to $12.3 billion in 2014, with $11.3 billion of that total coming from spending on newly introduced hepatitis C drugs.[59] Medicare Part D spent $4.5 billion on new hepatitis C medications in 2014, compared with $286 million that the program spent on earlier-generation hepatitis C drugs in 2013.[60]

Specialty drug spending in private and public health plans has been concentrated on a relatively narrow range of therapy areas including oncology, autoimmune diseases, HIV/AIDs, multiple sclerosis, hepatitis C, growth factors, and hormones for red cell production.[61]

For many insurers, the comparatively small share of enrollees who use specialty drugs accounts for a disproportionately large share of total prescription drug spending. For example, in Medicare Part D, specialty tier drugs made up 0.25% of prescriptions filled by enrollees in 2015 but more than 11% of total Part D drug spending.[62] In the private sector, PBM Prime Therapeutics estimated that specialty prescriptions made up less than one-half of 1% of commercial insurance claims in 2013 but 20% of pharmacy benefit spending for the Blue Cross and Blue Shield plans it served. According to CVS Caremark, 3.6% of its enrollees in the health plans it served used specialty drugs in 2013, which accounted for 20% of prescription drug spending at retail pharmacies and nearly the same share of pharmacy spending in hospitals and other institutions.[63]

Health care payers have been scrambling to adjust to the changing drug marketplace. For example, health care actuaries have been having difficulty projecting future costs for specialty drugs, which in turn affects insurers' ability to accurately bid to offer prescription drug coverage to consumers.[64]

COSTS AND BENEFITS OF SPECIALTY DRUGS

Manufacturers justify specialty drug prices based on the cost of bringing a new product to market and the potential benefits of the drugs. Specialty pharmaceuticals may improve a patient's quality of life or provide a cure, which, in turn, can provide offsetting savings to the health care system by way of fewer hospitalizations and other medical procedures.

Although publicly traded pharmaceutical manufacturers release information regarding aggregate company research and development spending, detailed information on the costs of developing specific drugs generally is not readily available. An oft-cited study put the average cost of developing a new prescription drug at about $802 million in 2001. The study was updated in 2014 to a cost of $2.6 billion.[65] There has been considerable debate among researchers about the estimate,[66] with a number of analysts saying that the true cost is likely to be lower.[67] Further, development costs for different drugs vary.[68]

Some targeted studies have looked at the costs and benefits of specific biologic and high-cost drugs. For example, a 2008 study found that using biologic drugs to treat rheumatoid arthritis and multiple sclerosis reduced the use of some other types of medical services. In this case, the savings did not offset the full cost of the drugs.[69] A study of biologics used to treat colorectal cancer indicated that the drugs improved outcomes and life expectancy but created large increases in total expenditures and did not substitute for other medical services.[70]

A recent study[71] examined the benefit-cost ratio of Sovaldi and another specialty hepatitis C drug, Harvoni. The study, which assumed an 11% average price discount for the drugs across payers,[72] found that the drugs, which can provide a cure, were cost-effective in selected patient groups at a threshold where each additional quality-of-life year was valued at $50,000 and were cost-effective for most patients at a $100,000 threshold.[73] However, the study noted that the resources needed to treat a large number of eligible patients could be "immense and unsustainable."

Recent research indicates that the price of new cancer therapies, many of which are specialty drugs, increased by 10% a year (adjusted for inflation and health benefits) from 1995 to 2013. The authors posit that manufacturers were able to set the prices of new products at or slightly above the prices of existing therapies. Government-required rebates and other discounts may have contributed to higher launch prices as manufacturers tried to make up for the discounts by raising prices in other parts of the market.[74]

There are increased efforts to provide research on the possible benefits and costs of specialty drugs. During the next two years, for example, the Institute for Clinical and Economic Review plans to produce 15 to 20 public reports on newly approved FDA high-impact drugs. The reports will analyze the drugs' comparative effectiveness, cost-effectiveness, and potential budget impact.[75]

SPECIALTY DRUG SPENDING CONTROLS

Private employers and insurers are the nation's largest purchasers of prescription drugs, accounting for a projected 43% of annual spending in 2013, followed by the federal and state governments at about 41% and consumer out-of-pocket spending at about 16%. (See **Figure 3** for prescription drug spending by source.) The health payers use a variety of strategies to control specialty drug spending.

Enrollee Utilization Policies

Health care payers pass on a portion of specialty drug costs to enrollees through plan premiums and annual deductibles.[76] Many payers also use targeted management tools including (1) requiring enrollees to pay higher cost sharing for expensive drugs (tiered formularies); (2) requiring prior authorization before covering certain medications; (3) mandating that enrollees try a less expensive drug before moving to a more expensive prescription product (step therapy); (4) limiting the length of an initial prescription to assess whether a drug works as intended; (5) requiring use of a specialty pharmacy; (6) offering only a limited formulary; (7) moving a drug to a pharmacy (retail) benefit from an institutional (medical) benefit to cut overhead; and (8) requiring closer oversight and monitoring of patients using specialty drugs.[77] (See Figure 4.)

This report will look at some of the most commonly used strategies.

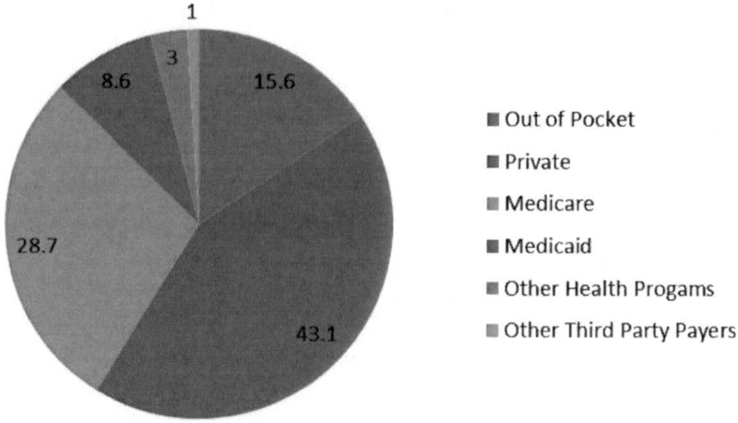

Source: Centers for Medicare & Medicaid Services, Office of the Actuary, *National Health Expenditures 2014- 2024*, Table 11.

Notes: The category *other health programs* includes the state Children's Health Insurance Program, Department of Defense, and Department of Veterans Affairs. *Other third party payers* includes worksite health care, other private revenues, Indian Health Service, workers' compensation, general assistance, maternal and child health, vocational rehabilitation, other federal programs, Substance Abuse and Mental Health Services Administration, other state and local programs, and school health.

Figure 3. 2014 U.S. Spending for Prescription Drugs by Source (by percentage of total spending).

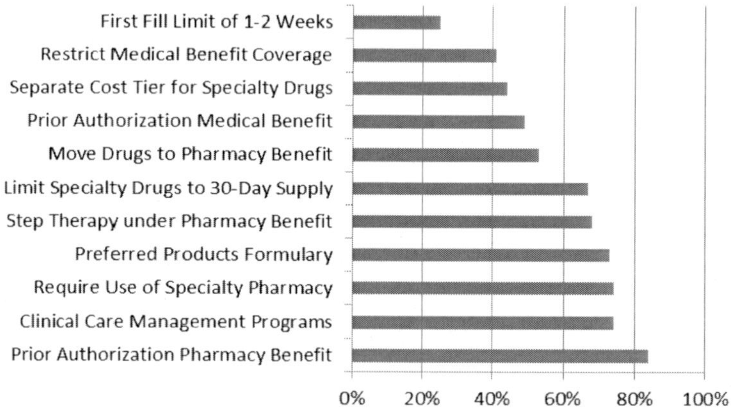

Source: Walgreens/Pharmacy Benefit Management Institute, *2013 Specialty Drug Benefit Report*.

Note: Based on survey of insurers and other plan sponsors covering 17.6 million enrollees.

Figure 4. Percentage of Insurers Using Strategies for Managing Specialty Drug Use (2012 commercial insurance plan data).

Tiered Formularies

Payers commonly include tiered pricing to induce enrollees to use drugs that are less expensive or that are considered more effective. Under tiered pricing, a generic or preferred brand-name drug[78] is put on a tier that requires a comparatively low co-payment, and drugs that are more expensive or deemed less effective are put on tiers requiring comparatively higher co-payments or coinsurance. In 2014, 80% of consumers with employer-sponsored insurance were in plans with three or more drug tiers, and 20% were in plans with four or more tiers.[79]

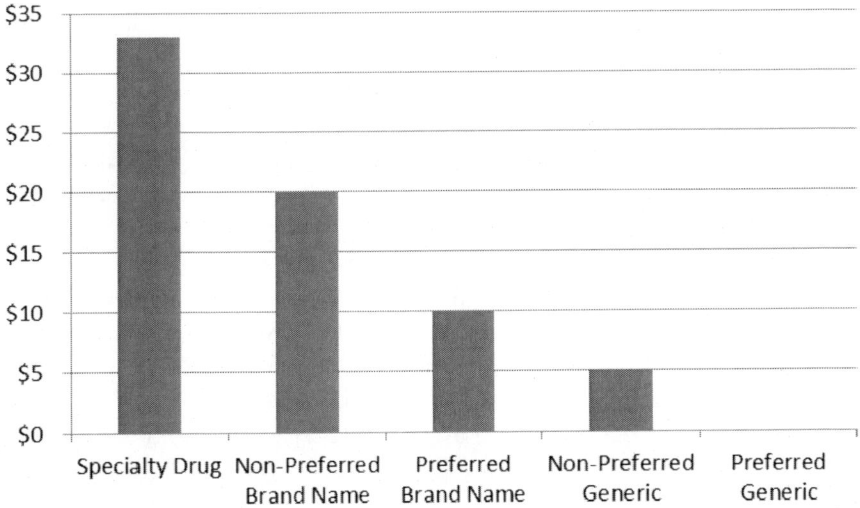

Source: CRS.

Notes: For purposes of this graphic, the preferred generic tier has a $0 co-payment; non-preferred generics have a $5 co-payment, preferred brand names have a $10 co-payment, non-preferred brand names have a $20 co-payment, and specialty drugs have 33% coinsurance.

Figure 5. Tiered Formulary; (example of pricing under a tiered formulary for a drug with a $ 100 price tag).

Payers often place specialty drugs on a tier that requires enrollees to pay coinsurance rather than a co-payment, which helps the payer keep pace with price inflation for expensive drugs and discourages use of the drugs in cases where substitutes are available.[80] For example, a payer could impose a flat $20 co-payment for a $100 drug or it could charge 33% coinsurance for the product, which would result in $33 in out-of-pocket spending.[81] Over time, the cost differential between price tiers has widened, imposing a greater burden on enrollees prescribed higher-priced drugs.[82]

While many consumers focus on the cost of monthly premiums when deciding whether a health plan is affordable, prescription drug tiers can have a major impact on the total cost of coverage. A recent analysis of non-group health plans[83] sold through ACA insurance exchanges[84] found that 60% of the least-comprehensive Bronze plans imposed co-insurance of 30% or more for drugs on specialty tiers, with 25% requiring coinsurance of 50% or more.[85] About 23% percent of Silver plans, which cover a larger share of the federally required benefits, still had specialty-tier coinsurance of 30% of more, as did 33% of Gold plans and 10% of the most expansive Platinum plans.[86] A few plans concentrated all drugs for treating certain conditions on a specialty tier that imposed coinsurance requirements, including not just the highest-cost drugs but also less expensive drugs used to treat the conditions, raising concerns about possible discrimination against certain classes of enrollees.[87] In addition, the plans may require beneficiaries to meet a deductible before covering prescription drugs.

A number of studies have shown that when insurers impose higher cost sharing for prescription drugs, fewer enrollees fill or continue their prescriptions.[88] There is some evidence that higher cost sharing does not affect prescription adherence for specialty drugs as much it does for traditional drugs. A 2006 analysis of 50 commercial health plans found that increases in specialty drug cost sharing reduced usage by 1%-21%, compared with a 25%-45% reduction for traditional drugs.[89] A separate review analyzed private health insurance claims for biologic drugs used to treat rheumatoid arthritis. If insurers doubled the average out-of-pocket payment for the arthritis treatment, the odds that a person would not use the drugs increased by about 9%. Consumers were much more likely not to fill or not to complete a prescription for traditional drugs when out-of-pocket payments doubled.[90]

Prescription Drug Coupons

Pharmaceutical manufacturers try to mitigate the impact of tiered formularies on consumers by offering drug coupons that reduce or eliminate required co-payments or coinsurance. Manufacturers may offer their coupons through their websites, in magazines and other media, or through a physician's office. A manufacturer might offer a coupon that limits a consumer's co-payment to $50 for a drug that has a negotiated price of $500, even if the consumer's health plan requires a $150 co-payment. In this case, the manufacturer provides a $100 subsidy to cover the difference between the coupon price limit and the co-payment amount.

Coupons appear to be particularly important for consumers using specialty drugs. PBM Prime Therapeutics found the insurance beneficiaries it served used manufacturer coupons to cover $21.2 million out of a total of $35.3 million in annual out-of-pocket costs for specialty drugs in 2013.[91] The beneficiaries used coupons to reduce the average out-of-pocket spending for anti-inflammatory drugs by nearly 77% and to realize nearly 61% in savings on drugs for treating multiple sclerosis. The coupons helped increase prescription adherence (whether patients take their drugs as prescribed, such as three times daily, and whether they continue the full course of treatment). However, because the coupons were very effective in lowering required co-payments, they also may have induced some consumers to use more expensive drugs when less expensive substitutes may have been available, according to the study.

Some health payers and PBMs prohibit enrollees from using coupons for certain drugs.[92] Pharmaceutical manufacturers may be liable under the federal anti-kickback statute if they offer coupons to induce consumers to purchase their companies' products under federal programs, such as the Medicare Part D prescription drug benefit. The federal anti-kickback statute[93] makes it a felony for a person to knowingly and willfully offer, pay, solicit, or receive anything of value (i.e., *remuneration*) in return for a referral or to induce generation of business reimbursable under a federal health care program.

Site of Care

Individuals covered by health insurance may obtain prescription drugs through their plan's pharmacy benefit (which covers outpatient prescriptions filled in drug stores) or through its medical benefit (which covers drugs administered by a health care provider in an institutional setting—such as a hospital outpatient center, a doctor's office, a freestanding infusion center—or in a patient's home by a special provider). As a general rule of thumb, oral drugs often are covered under a pharmacy benefit whereas infused or injected drugs, such as infused oncology drugs, are covered under a medical benefit.

According to analytics and consulting firm Artemetrx, about half of total specialty drug spending reported by commercial insurers is processed through the pharmacy benefit and half is processed through the medical benefit.[94] A number of consultants say this dual system can make it more difficult to track and control spending on specialty drugs. Because of technical differences in drug coding and reporting under the two systems, a health insurer may have difficulty monitoring the total regimen of drugs used for a patient. Insurers also may have difficulty imposing utilization controls, such as requiring prior authorization, for drugs purchased by and administered in a physician's office.[95]

In an effort to control drug spending, some insurers have moved to coordinated drug benefits.[96] Some studies caution that potential cost savings from integrating the pharmacy and medical benefits may have been oversold. A recent analysis by Artemetrx found that prices for certain drugs actually were lower when the drugs were dispensed in a physician's office.[97] From the consumer perspective, out-of-pocket costs may be higher when a drug is covered under a tiered pharmacy benefit rather than as part of a medical service. For example, an insurer may charge 33% coinsurance under the pharmacy benefit, as opposed to a smaller, flat co-payment for a drug provided as part of a medical benefit. That has become an issue as more specialty drugs, particularly cancer drugs, are offered in oral form rather than as infused products. Dozens of states have passed laws to prohibit insurers from imposing higher out-of-pocket payments for oral cancer drugs purchased at a pharmacy than for similar infused products delivered in a medical setting.[98]

Specialty Pharmacies

Specialty drugs often are distributed through specialty pharmacies[99] that offer a range of services beyond distribution or sale, including helping to administer complex drugs that must be infused or that can have serious side effects, performing patient education, and monitoring patients' reactions to prescribed medications. Specialty pharmacies may handle paperwork associated with insurer reimbursement, manufacturer data reporting, and FDA reporting requirements. Insurers use specialty pharmacies to more closely monitor and counsel patients during a course of treatment to improve medication adherence, which is a major concern given the high cost of many specialty drugs.

A number of PBMs and insurers have purchased specialty pharmacies, and some require that the insured beneficiaries they serve fill their prescriptions through those pharmacies. Payers may be able to secure better prices through their own specialty distribution system and to monitor enrollee outcomes more closely. Some drug manufacturers have contracted directly with a limited number of specialty pharmacies to limit distribution and better control the supply chain.[100]

Manufacturer-Payer Negotiations

Even though pharmaceutical manufacturers announce a price for newly developed drugs, the actual price paid is likely to vary among public and private health care payers, which in turn affects how much insured consumers pay out of pocket and the level of government and private insurer spending for a product.

In the private sector (and in some government programs), insurers and other payers and the PBMs with which they contract negotiate price concessions with manufacturers. Private health payers secure rebates from manufacturers based on the volume of drugs their enrollees are predicted to use, for example. Larger payers with a higher volume of prescription activity are likely to secure more generous rebates. Insurers and PBMs may receive a price reduction if they include a single manufacturer's drug on their formulary, while excluding competing drugs.[101] Payers may secure price concessions if they put a drug on a tier that carries a lower co-payment or coinsurance than other, similar drugs. However, in the case of specialty drugs that have few substitutes, payers may have less leverage to negotiate, at least initially.[102]

In addition to private-sector negotiations, U.S. government agencies operate a range of payment systems across and within health care programs. Among the public payer systems,

- The state-federal Medicaid program requires participating drug manufacturers to provide a minimum 23.1% price rebate to the government for innovator drugs[103] and limits annual price increases for prescription products to the rate of consumer inflation.[104] To participate in Medicaid, manufacturers must take part in the 340B Drug Pricing Program, which requires discounts on outpatient drugs to eligible health care organizations and entities.[105]
- The Veterans Health Administration (VA) operates a centralized system for buying drugs, including a central formulary.[106] The Department of Defense (DOD) and the VA use certain federal pricing arrangements for these direct purchases, including Federal Supply Schedule prices and prices available to the four largest federal purchasers. Prime vendors used by DOD and VA provide a fixed percentage discount off the lowest price otherwise available for each drug.
- The Medicare Part D program prohibits the Secretary of Health and Human Services (HHS) from negotiating drug prices with

manufacturers or creating a set formulary.[107] Part D private insurers, often working through PBMs, negotiate drug prices and administer benefits. Manufacturers must provide a 50% discount for brand-name drugs purchased by enrollees who have reached the Part D "doughnut hole," or coverage gap.[108]

Prices for brand-name prescription drugs often are higher in the United States than in European and other countries that have government-run health care systems, including a centralized mechanism for pricing and purchasing drugs.[109]

Sovaldi as Case Study of Payer Negotiations

The introduction of specialty drugs for treating hepatitis C provides an example of payer-manufacturer negotiations. In late 2013, drug maker Gilead received FDA approval for Sovaldi, a drug that offers a high cure rate for hepatitis C patients, and brought it to the market at a list price of $84,000 for a 12-week course of treatment.[110] Sovaldi's initial price was not as high as for some other specialty drugs. Whereas many specialty drugs are targeted at a narrow population, an estimated 3.2 million Americans are infected with the hepatitis C virus.[111] Private and public health payers faced the prospect of billions of dollars in up-front costs for Sovaldi, as compared with other treatments. Although the drug is expected to produce some long-term cost savings by way of reduced hospitalizations or other services, there are uncertainties about the size and timing of the reductions.[112] Further, many U.S. consumers may switch health insurance plans on an annual basis, meaning one insurer could bear the entire up-front cost of Sovaldi for an enrollee who then moved to another health plan, which then could benefit from the fact that the individual did not face ongoing medical costs for treating hepatitis C.

Public and private payers have tried to limit spending for the drug by restricting coverage for Sovaldi to those in advanced stages of the disease and requiring prior authorization, including proof that a prospective patient has not used drugs or alcohol for a certain period of time.[113] Payers entered into price negotiations with the manufacturer, Gilead, and some imposed mandatory price reductions (i.e., Medicaid requires mandatory new drug rebates of at least 23.1%, and many state Medicaid programs imposed additional controls such as prior authorization requirements).[114] Gilead also offered discount coupons for insured patients and other assistance for certain uninsured patients.[115] Gilead has said that its average discount for Sovaldi was 22% in

2014.[116] In addition to reductions in the U.S. market, Gilead provided deep discounts to payers, including government programs, in other countries.[117]

In October 2014, Gilead secured FDA approval for a second hepatitis C therapy called Harvoni, which it initially priced at around $94,000.[118] In December 2014, manufacturer Abbvie secured FDA approval for a competing hepatitis C drug called Viekira Pak, which it initially priced at $83,319.[119] As competition emerged, payers became more aggressive in price negotiations. PBM Express Scripts announced that Viekira Pak would be its exclusive option for specialty drugs to treat hepatitis C patients starting January 1, 2015.[120] Gilead secured contracts with other PBMs and payers for its drugs, but company executives said in a February 2015 conference call that they expected to provide average price discounts of about 46% on their hepatitis C drugs in 2015, compared with the average 22% discounts in 2014.[121]

OUTSTANDING ISSUES

Consumer Insurance Coverage of Specialty Drugs

One of the thorniest issues facing health care payers is how to control specialty drug spending without restricting coverage to the point that some insured enrollees cannot afford needed drugs. Public and private payers say that utilization strategies such as tiered pricing merely provide an incentive for consumers to use less expensive or more effective drugs. However, many specialty therapies are one-of-a-kind products with no ready substitutes, meaning that tiered pricing mainly serves to increase cost sharing for enrollees prescribed such drugs (thus lowering plan spending).[122] That outcome, in turn, can affect health outcomes given studies showing that drug adherence diminishes as price sharing increases.

Recent data indicate that a small share of consumers face high cost sharing for drugs. In 2013, more than half of retail prescriptions filled by all insured consumers cost $5 or less and 20% had no co-payment, including many generics.[123] At the same time, about 2% of prescriptions had co-payments or coinsurance of $70 or more and accounted for nearly 30% of consumer out-of-pocket spending for drugs.[124]

Consumer and health care advocacy groups have charged that some health payers use tiered pricing and formulary management to discourage people with expensive conditions from enrolling in their plans. A coalition of civil rights and AIDS groups filed a lawsuit in Florida in July 2014 charging that four insurers offering coverage through the state's ACA exchange had placed all HIV/AIDS drugs, including generics, on their highest-priced tier, effectively discouraging people with AIDS from buying their policies.[125] State officials negotiated an agreement with one of the insurers under which it agreed to alter drug pricing.[126] A recent study of HIV/AIDS drug pricing in 12 state ACA marketplaces found evidence of potentially discriminatory use of price tiers in 12 of 48 studied insurance plans.[127] In February 2015, CMS published rules that set more stringent standards for individual and small-group insurance plan formularies[128] and warned private insurers that placing most or all drugs for treating a specific condition on the highest cost tiers effectively could discriminate against individuals with those conditions.[129]

In addition, legislation has been introduced at the state level to require "transparency" in drug pricing by requiring manufacturers to provide information on the cost of developing a certain drug, and the rationale used to set the price for the product.[130]

In Congress, lawmakers have introduced legislation to allow beneficiaries to seek an exception for drugs placed on Part D specialty price tiers and to amend federal law so that health plans provide no less favorable coverage for oral or self-injectable cancer drugs used on an outpatient basis as for traditional chemotherapy administered in a health care setting.[131] At the state level, dozens of legislatures have debated or enacted legislation to prohibit specialty drug tiers in insurance plans and to limit co-payments and other out-of-pocket costs for specialty drugs.[132] For example, a 2014 Maryland law prohibits insurers from imposing a co-payment or coinsurance for a covered drug that exceeds $150 for a 30-day supply.[133]

Although such proposals provide financial relief to individual consumers, they do not address the overall price of drugs or total spending for the products. Rather, the legislation may shift more of the cost of the drugs on to private and public payers. Those payers, in turn, may then pass on the costs to all enrollees in the form of higher monthly premiums or plan deductibles.

Health care analysts have suggested other approaches to managing specialty drugs that might help to improve patient outcomes and manage costs such as value-based purchasing.[134]

Potential Changes in Drug Payment and Pricing

Health care analysts have recommended various ways to give payers more power to negotiate, impose lower prices for specialty drugs, or make the drug purchasing system more cost-effective in terms of linking drug payments to the efficacy of treatments.

On the government side, lawmakers have introduced legislation that would impose Medicaid rebates on drugs purchased by low-income beneficiaries in the Medicare Part D program, including specialty drugs. President Obama's FY2016 budget proposal recommends that the Secretary of HHS be allowed to negotiate directly with manufacturers to set Medicare Part D prices for biologics and other high-cost drugs that are eligible for specialty tier placement. Pharmaceutical manufacturers seeking to participate in Part D would be required to supply HHS with data and information necessary to come to a price agreement on specialty drugs.[135]

Some analysts have suggested new payment models that would allow insurers to spread the cost of expensive drugs over a period of time. One example would be to create a new credit system with a third party providing loans or insurance to payers.[136]

Certain medical professional organizations, led by oncology specialists, and some health insurers have said they will begin using more rigorous economic cost-benefit analyses to determine which drugs to cover and prescribe.[137] Other health analysts contend that a growing body of data obtained from electronic health records and additional information systems could be used to help rationalize the drug payment system as described below.

At a recent symposium, the IMS Institute for Health Care Informatics, which has the nation's largest database of pharmacy claims and other prescription drug data, suggested tapping a rapidly growing body of online health care data to examine possible new ways to price drugs and other breakthrough therapies.[138] Possible ideas include paying different prices for drugs depending on how they are used and how well they perform.[139] Another option would be to have the federal government provide conditional approval and pricing for a drug that could be adjusted depending on whether it performed as intended. Patient use, outcomes, and treatment costs could be tracked through electronic health record systems.[140] A number of European countries use similar models.[141]

End Notes

[1] IMS Institute for Healthcare Informatics, *Medicine Use and Shifting Costs of Healthcare: A Review of the Use of Medicines in the U.S. in 2013*, April 2014, p. 40; at http://www.imshealth.com/portal/site/imshealth/menuitem.762a961826aad98f53c753c71ad8c22a/?vgnextoid=2684d47626745410VgnVCM10000076192ca2RCRD IMS Institute,

Medicines Use and Spending Shifts: A Review of the Use of Medicines in the U.S. in 2014, April 2015, p. 8, at http://www.imshealth. com/portal/site/imshealth/menuitem.762a961826 aad98f53c753c71ad8c22a/?vgnextoid=3f140a4331e8c410VgnVCM1000000e2e2ca2RCRD &vgnextchannel=736de5fda637041 0VgnVCM10000076192ca2RCRD&vgnextfmt= default; and United-Healthcare Center for Health Reform & Modernization, *The Growth of Specialty Pharmacy: Current Trends and Future Opportunities*, April 2014, p.1, at http://www.unitedhealthgroup.com/Modernization/KeyIssues/SpecialtyPharmacy.aspx. U.S. health care spending grew by a projected 5.5% in 2014, while prescription drug spending rose 12.6%, driven by specialty drugs and increased prescription drug use. Centers for Medicare & Medicaid Services, N*ational Health Expenditure Projections 2014-2024*, p. 2, at http://www.cms.gov/Research-Statistics-Data-and-Systems/Statistics-Trends-andReports/ NationalHealthExpendData/Downloads/proj2014.pdf.

[2] CRS Report R41483, *Follow-On Biologics: The Law and Intellectual Property Issues*, by John R. Thomas. Also see "Biologics" below. By comparison, traditional drugs are chemically manufactured (small-molecule) substances that often come in tablet or capsule form.

[3] See "Orphan Drugs" below.

[4] IMS Institute, *Medicines Use and Spending Shifts: A Review of the Use of Medicines in the U.S. in 2014*, April 2015, p. 8. The IMS data are based on actual claims and spending by pharmacies, clinics, hospitals, and other health care providers. The data cover 100% of the retail and non-retail channels for national drug sales at actual transaction prices and are matched with other analytic tools used to track patient drug activity over time. IMS said prescription drug spending increased by 13% in 2014, the highest annual increase since 2001. The increase was driven by increased spending for specialty drugs and a slower pace of patent expirations for existing drugs, which can promote use of less expensive generic drugs.

[5] Pharmacy Benefits Manager (PBM) Catamaran, which manages prescription drug spending for 35 million enrollees in U.S. health plans offered by businesses and other health providers, recorded a 20% increase in specialty drug spending in 2014, compared with a 14.3% increase in 2013, driven by increased costs for hepatitis C drugs. Catamaran, *2015 Informed Trends: Moments of Opportunity*, April 2014, p. 16, at http://catamaranrx.com/ Insights/Trend-Report/. The data exclude some clients such as those in cash card, workers' compensation, state insurance exchanges, Medicaid, and Medicare Part D. PBM Express Scripts said that specialty drug costs among its commercially insured members rose by about 17% annually on average from 2010 to 2013. In 2014, traditional drug spending for commercially insured members rose by 6.4% and spending for specialty drugs rose by 30.9%, for an overall increase of 13.1%. Express Scripts, *The 2014 Drug Trend Report*, March 2015, p. 11, at http://lab.express-scripts.com/drug-trend-report. Trend and other measures are calculated separately for those members with commercial insurance coverage, and for Medicaid and for Medicare beneficiaries. The analysis does not include drugs billed through the medical benefit (treatment offered in a health care setting such as a physician's office) rather than the pharmacy benefit of an insurance plan.

[6] See text box entitled "What is a Pharmacy Benefit Manager?"

[7] For example, see Express Scripts, "U.S. Rx Spending Increased 13.1% in 2014," March 10, 2015, at http://lab.express-scripts.com/insights/industry-updates/us-rx-spending-increased-13-percent-in-2014. Express Scripts said specialty drugs made up 31.8% of drug spending in 2014.

[8] The findings are based on data from both prescription drug pharmacy claims and medical claims. Artemetrx, *An Evaluation of Specialty Drug Pricing Under the Pharmacy and*

Medical Benefit, March 2014, p. 3, at http://www.artemetrx.com/wp-content/uploads/2014/08/artemetrx-evaluation-of-specialty-drug-pricing.pdf; and Prime Therapeutics, "Specialty Drugs are Forecasted to be 50% of All Drug Expenditures in 2018," April 4, 2013, at http://cdn2.content.compendiumblog.com/uploads/user/e7c690e8-6ff9-102a-ac6d-e4aebca50425/accf0d87-0d14-4aa7-bbf3-193b90c8d68c/File/1f8476 cb4a60eb472893ddf 381c9c3ec/prediction_that_by_2018__more_than_50_percent_of_all_ drug_expenditures_ will_be_specialty.pdf. The Prime Therapeutics data encompass drug spending through both pharmacy claims and medical claims for 6.8 million commercially insured beneficiaries.

[9] For example, the number of patients starting treatment with specialty hepatitis C medications rose from 17,000 in 2013 to 161,000 in 2014, according to the IMS Institute, *Medicines Use and Spending Shifts: A Review of the Use of Medicines in the U.S. in 2014*, April 2015, p. 10.

[10] Leah Goddard, *Pharmacy Benefit Management in the US*, IBISWorld Industry Report OD4620, July 2015.

[11] For more background on PBMs, see U.S. Department of Labor, "2014 ERISA Council PBM Compensation and Fee Disclosure," at http://www.dol.gov/ebsa/publications/2014ACreport1.html#4.

[12] *Business Wire*, "Rite Aid Completes Acquisition of Leading Independent Pharmacy Benefit Manager (PBM) EnvisionRx," June 24, 2015, at http://www.businesswire.com/news/home/20150624005906/en/Rite-Aid-CompletesAcquisition-Leading-Independent-Pharmacy#.VbuGqvmZOew.

[13] Optum, "OptumRx, Catamaran Complete Combination," July 23, 2015, at https://www.optum.com/news-events/news/optumrx-catamaran-complete-combination. html.

[14] Medicare is an entitlement program that provides health insurance to individuals aged 65 and older, and it has been expanded over the years to include certain disabled individuals under the age of 65. Medicaid is a state-federal, means-tested entitlement program that finances the delivery of primary and acute medical services as well as long-term services and supports. The Veterans Health Administration (VHA), within the Department of Veterans Affairs (VA), operates the nation's largest integrated health care delivery system to provide care for veteran patients.

[15] See "Costs and Benefits of Specialty Drugs."

[16] National Health Law Program, "NHeLP and The AIDS Institute File HIV/AIDS Discrimination Complaint Against Florida Health Insurers," press release, May 29, 2014, at http://www.healthlaw.org/news/press-releases/224-nhelp-andthe-aids-institute-file-hivaids-discrimination-complaint-against-florida-health-insurers. Caroline Pearson, Avalere Health, "Exchange Plans Increase Costs of Specialty Drugs for Patients in 2015," press release, December 2, 2014, at http://avalere.com/news/exchange-plans-increase-costs-of-specialty-drugs-for-patients-in-2015.

[17] The Medicare Prescription Drug, Improvement, and Modernization Act of 2003 (MMA; P.L. 108-173). Medicare Part D is a voluntary program under which private insurers bid to offer prescription drug benefits to Medicare enrollees. Although the MMA was passed in 2003, Part D did not take full effect until 2006.

[18] CRS Report R43778, *Medicaid Prescription Drug Pricing and Policy*, by Cliff Binder.

[19] Centers for Medicare & Medicaid Services (CMS), *National Health Expenditure Accounts, Historical Tables*, at http://www.cms.gov/Research-Statistics-Data-and-Systems/Statistics-Trends-and-Reports/NationalHealthExpendData/NationalHealthAccountsHistorical.html.

[20] CRS Report R41114, *The Hatch-Waxman Act: Over a Quarter Century Later*, by Wendy H. Schacht and John R. Thomas.

[21] CRS Report R41483, *Follow-On Biologics: The Law and Intellectual Property Issues*, by John R. Thomas.

[22] CRS Report R41705, *The National Institutes of Health (NIH): Background and Congressional Issues*, by Judith A. Johnson; and CRS Report CRS Report RL32324, *Federal R&D, Drug Discovery, and Pricing: Insights from the NIHUniversity-Industry Relationship*, by Wendy H. Schacht.

[23] CRS Report RL31181, *Research Tax Credit: Current Law and Policy Issues for the 114th Congress*, by Gary Guenther.

[24] The U.S. Food and Drug Administration (FDA) defines a brand-name drug as a drug marketed under a proprietary, trademark-protected name. Generic drugs are identical to traditional brand-name drugs in dosage, safety, strength, route of administration, quality, performance characteristics, and intended use.

[25] Examples of such legislation in the 114th Congress include H.R. 2739, S. 1566, and H.R. 1600.

[26] Health insurance is mainly regulated by the states. See Alex Wayne, "Drugmakers Turn Heat on Insurers by Backing Copay Limits," *Bloomberg*, March 12, 2015, at http://www. bloomberg.com/news/articles/2015-03-12/drugmakersturn-heat-on-insurers-by-backing-copay-limits-health;and Patrick Connole, "States Target Prescription Drugs in 'Cap The Copay' Bills; Analysts Warn of Offsets," *AIS Health*, April 20, 2015, at http://aishealth. com/archive/nhpw042015 02.

[27] Michelle Andrews, "Some States Mandate Better Coverage of Oral Cancer Drugs," *Kaiser Health News*, May 14, 2012, at http://www.kaiserhealthnews.org/features/insuring-your-health/2012/cancer-drugs-by-pill-instead-of-ivmichelle-andrews-051512.aspx; and Bo Wang, Steven Joffe, and Aaron Kesselheim,"Chemotherapy Parity Laws: A Remedy for High Drug Costs?," *JAMA Internal Medicine*, November 2014, at http://archinte. jamanetwork.com/article.aspx?articleid=1907003.

[28] Covered California, "Covered California Board Protects Consumers Against Skyrocketing Specialty Drug Costs To Ensure Access To Vital Medications," May 21, 2015, http://news.coveredca.com/2015/05/covered-california-boardprotects.html.

[29] IMS Institute for Health Informatics, *Global Outlook for Medicines Through 2018*, November 2014, p. 1, at http://www.imshealth.com/portal/site/imshealth/menuitem.762a961826aad 98f53c753c71ad8c22a/?vgnextoid= 266e05267aea9410VgnVCM10000076192ca2RCRD.

[30] CMS, *National Health Expenditure Projections, 2014-2024- Tables,* Table 2, at https://www. cms.gov/ResearchStatistics-Data-and-Systems/Statistics-Trends-and-Reports/NationalHealthExpendData/NationalHealthAccountsProjected.html. The United States is projected to spend $305 billion on prescription drugs in 2014, out of total health care spending of about $3.08 trillion. The National Health Expenditure estimates are based on U.S. Census Bureau and IMS drug data. The figures include retail sales of prescription drugs, subtract manufacturer rebates, and add in government spending for drugs provided by government-owned mail-order facilities. They do not include drugs dispensed in institutional settings such as hospitals or clinics. See "National Health Expenditure Accounts Methodology Paper 2010: Definitions, Sources and Methods," at http://www. cms.gov/Research-StatisticsData-and-Systems/Statistics-Trends-and-Reports/NationalHealthExpendData/downloads/dsm-10.pdf.

[31] CMS, *National Health Expenditure Projections, 2014-2024* and *Historical Data,* at http://www.cms.gov/ResearchStatistics-Data-and-Systems/Statistics-Trends-and-Reports/NationalHealthExpendData/NationalHealthAccountsProjected.html. For additional background, see Centers for Disease Control, *Health United States 2013*, May 14, 2014, p. 30, at http://www.cdc.gov/nchs/data/hus/hus13.pdf#listfigures. By comparison, overall

health care spending grew by a forecast 5.5% in 2014, with hospital services growing by 4.4% and physician and clinical services growing by 4.8%.

[32] CMS, *National Health Expenditure Projections, 2014-2024,* Table 11, at http://www.cms.gov/ Research-StatisticsData-and-Systems/Statistics-Trends-and-Reports/NationalHealthExpendData/NationalHealthAccountsProjected.html. For additional analysis of prescription drug spending, see Glen Schumock, Edward Li, Katie Suda, Linda Matusiak, Robert Hunkler, Lee Vermeulen, and James Hoffman, "National Trends in Prescription Drug Expenditures and Projections for 2014," *American Journal of Health-System Pharmacy*, vol. 71 (2014), pp. 6-23, at http://www.ashpmedia.org/AJHP/Drug Expenditures-2014.pdf.

[33] Prescription drug demand declined after the onset of the 2007 recession and recovered slowly. IMS Institute for Healthcare Informatics, *Medicine Use and Shifting Costs of Healthcare: A Review of the Use of Medicines in the U.S. in 2013*, April 2014, p. 7, at http://www. imshealth.com/portal/site/imshealth/menuitem.762a961826aad98f53c753c71 ad8c22a/?vgnextoid=2684d47626745410VgnVCM10000076192ca2RCRD.See also Andrea Sisko, et al., "National Health Expenditure Projections, 2013–23: Faster Growth Expected With Expanded Coverage And Improving Economy," *Health Affairs*, vol. 33, no. 10 (October 2014), pp. 1-10.

[34] IMS Institute for Healthcare Informatics, "M*edicine Use and Spending Shifts: A Review of the Use of Medicines in the U.S. in 2014*, April 2015, p. 6, at http://www.imshealth.com/ portal/site/imshealth/menuitem.762a961826aad98f53c753c71ad8c22a/?vgnextoid= 2684d47626745410VgnVCM10000076192ca2RCRD. Over the past several years, patents for a record number of top-selling traditional drugs expired, a situation that market analysts dubbed the *patent cliff.* The patent expirations paved the way for manufacturers to market an array of new generic substitutes, helping to hold down overall drug prices.

[35] FDA, "Understanding Generic Drugs," at http://www.fda.gov/Drugs/ResourcesForYou/ Consumers/BuyingUsingMedicineSafely/UnderstandingGenericDrugs/.

[36] CRS Report R41114, *The Hatch-Waxman Act: Over a Quarter Century Later*, by Wendy H. Schacht and John R. Thomas.

[37] Congressional Budget Office, *Effects of Using Generic Drugs on Medicare's Prescription Drug Spending*, September 15, 2010, at https://www.cbo.gov/publication/21800.

[38] CMS, *National Health Expenditure Projections, 2014-2024, Forecast Summary*, at http://www.cms.gov/ResearchStatistics-Data-and-Systems/Statistics-Trends-and-Reports/NationalHealthExpendData/Downloads/proj2014.pdf. By comparison, overall health care spending grew by a forecast 5.5% in 2014, with hospital services growing by 4.4% and physician and clinical services growing by 4.8%.

[39] See CRS Report R42663, *Health Insurance Exchanges Under the Patient Protection and Affordable Care Act (ACA)*, by Bernadette Fernandez and Annie L. Mach. Patient Protection and Affordable Care Act (ACA; P.L. 111-148, as amended) coverage was effective January 1, 2014. The ACA also expanded the Medicare Part D benefit. CRS Report R41196, *Medicare Provisions in the Patient Protection and Affordable Care Act (PPACA): Summary and Timeline*, coordinated by Patricia A. Davis.

[40] Catamaran, *2015 Informed Trends: Moments of Opportunity*, April, 2014, at http:// catamaranrx.com/Insights/TrendReport/.

[41] Senate Committee on Health, Education, Labor and Pensions, Subcommittee on Primary Health and Aging, "Why Are Some Generic Drugs Skyrocketing in Price," November 20, 2014, at http://www.help.senate.gov/hearings/hearing/?id=a7beb0ef-5056-a032-521e-c63f76dda7f3.

[42] Gayle C. Johnston and Miguel Rodriguez, "The Facts, Figures and Trends in U.S. Pharmaceutical Distribution," Distribution Management Association's Center for Healthcare Supply Chain Research, powerpoint, March 8-11, 2015, p. 22, at http://www.hcsupplychainresearch.org/projects/pdfs/2012-SpecPharm-ExecSummary.pdf https://www.google.com/search?q=2013Specialty+Pharmaceuticals+Facts%2C+Figures+and+Trends+in+Healthcare&ie=utf-8&oe=utf-8.

[43] 42 C.F.R 423.578(a)(7). CMS regulations allow private insurers that offer Part D plans to place prescriptions with a negotiated price of $600 per month or more on a specialty price tier, where the insurers can charge enrollees up to 33% of the price of the drug. The $600 threshold was instituted in 2008 and has not been raised since that time. See CMS, "Medicare Part D Specialty Tier," April 2014, at http://www.cms.gov/Medicare/Prescription-Drug-Coverage/PrescriptionDrugCovGenIn/Downloads/SpecialtyTier Methodology.pdf. Also see "Tiered Formularies."

[44] Antibodies are proteins produced by the immune system in response to foreign proteins, or antigens. Monoclonal antibodies are developed to target specific antigens, such as those on cancer cells.

[45] FDA, "Overview of Biologic Products," webinar, at http://www.slideshare.net/robpuopolo/061713-biologicalproduct-fda-basics-webinar-2.

[46] *The Economist*, "Going Large," January 3, 2015, http://www.economist.com/news/business/21637387-wave-newmedicines-known-biologics-will-be-good-drugmakers-may-not-be-so-good; and Sarah Turk, IBISWorld Industry Report 32541, "Brand Name Pharmaceutical Manufacturing in the US," April 2015.

[47] For information see CRS Report R42890, *The Role of Patents and Regulatory Exclusivities in Pharmaceutical Innovation*, by John R. Thomas.

[48] CRS Report R41483, *Follow-On Biologics: The Law and Intellectual Property Issues*, by John R. Thomas.

[49] Ibid. A biosimilar is defined as a biological product if it is "highly similar to the reference product notwithstanding minor differences in clinically inactive components" and "there are no clinically meaningful differences between the [biosimilar] and the reference product in terms of safety, purity, and potency of the product." The ACA provides a period of exclusivity for manufacturers of certain biologic brand-name drugs and biosimilar products. (42.U.S.C. §262(i)(2).) The FDA has a major role in setting standards for biosimilar drugs and has begun the process of implementing the ACA provisions. See also FDA, "Biosimilars," at http://www.fda.gov/drugs/developmentapprovalprocess/howdrugsare developedandapproved/approvalapplications/therapeuticbiologicapplications/biosimilars/default.htm.

[50] Congressional Budget Office, "S. 1965: Biologics Price Competition and Innovation Act of 2007," at http://www.cbo.gov/sites/default/files/cbofiles/ftpdocs/94xx/doc9496/s1695.pdf; and Department of Health and Human Services, Office of the Assistant Secretary for Planning and Evaluation, *Expanding the Use of Generic Drugs*, December 2010, p. 10, at http://aspe.hhs.gov/sp/reports/2010/genericdrugs/ib.pdf.

[51] FDA, "Developing Products for Rare Diseases and Conditions," at http://www.fda.gov/ForIndustry/DevelopingProductsforRareDiseasesConditions/ucm 2005525.htm.

[52] CRS Report R42890, *The Role of Patents and Regulatory Exclusivities in Pharmaceutical Innovation*, by John R. Thomas.

[53] FDA, "CDER New Drug Review: 2014 Update," December 11, 2014, at http://www.fda.gov/AboutFDA/CentersOffices/OfficeofMedicalProductsandTobacco/CDER/ucm074833.

htmandhttp://www.fda.gov/Drugs/DevelopmentApprovalProcess/Drug Innovation/ucm 429873.htm.

[54] Catamaran, *2014 Informed Trends: Moments of Opportunity*, p. 13, April 16, 2014, p. 8, at https://trendreport.catamaranrx.com/Catamaran. According to the report, a sampling of orphan drugs launched from 2012 to 2013 found at least five with annual costs close to or exceeding $150,000 per patient. Costs for another three orphan drugs approached $300,000 or more per patient per year.

[55] Aaron Kesselheim, Jessica Myers, Daniel Solomon, Wolfgang Winkelmayer, Raisa Levin, and Jerry Avorn, "The Prevalence and Cost of Unapproved Uses of Top-Selling Orphan Drugs," *PLoS ONE*, vol. 7, no. 2 (February 21, 2012), at http://www.ncbi.nlm.nih.gov/pmc/ articles/PMC3283698/.

[56] EvaluatePharma, "Orphan Drug Report 2014," October 2014, at http://info. evaluategroup. com/rs/evaluatepharmaltd/images/2014OD.pdf; and Sara Reardon, "Regulators Adopt More Orphan Drugs," *Nature*, April 1, 2014, at http://www.nature. com/news/regulators-adopt-more-orphan-drugs-1.14970.

[57] IMS Institute for Healthcare Informatics, *Medicines Use and Spending Shifts: A Review of the Use of Medicines in the U.S. in 2014*, April 2015, p. 8.

[58] Express Scripts, *The 2014 Drug Trend Report*, March 2015, p. 11, at http://lab.express-scripts.com/drug-trend-report.

[59] IMS Institute for Healthcare Informatics, *Medicines Use and Spending Shifts: A Review of the Use of Medicines in the U.S. in 2014*, April 2015, pp. 8-9.

[60] Charles Ornstein, "New Hepatitis C Drugs are Costing Medicare Billions," *ProPublica,* March 29, 2015, reprinted in the *Washington Post* at http://www.washingtonpost.com/national/ health-science/medicare-spent-45-billion-on-newhepatitis-c-drugs-last-year-data-shows/2015/03/29/66952dde-d32a-11e4-a62f-ee745911a4ff_story.html.

[61] Waseem Noor and Michael Kleinrock, "Pharma 50 Insight: The Accelerating Growth of Specialty Markets," *Pharmaceutical Executive*, June 2014, at http://www.imshealth.com/ deployedfiles/consulting/Global/Content/How%20We%20Help/Strategy%20&%20 Portfolio/pharma50_2014.pdf.

[62] CMS, "Medicare Part D Specialty Tier," April 7, 2014, at http://www.cms.gov/ Medicare/Prescription-Drug-Coverage/PrescriptionDrugCovGenIn/Downloads/SpecialtyTierMethodology.pdf.

[63] See Prime Therapeutics, *Looking Back Moving Forward, 2014 Report on Prescription Drug Costs*, p. 14; and CVS Caremark, *Specialty Trend Management, Where to Go Next*, November 20, 2013, p. 3, at http://www.cvshealth.com/sites/default/files/Insights% 202013.pdf.

[64] American Academy of Actuaries, Letter to Centers on Medicare & Medicaid Services, November 11, 2014, at http://www.actuary.org/files/Medicaid_capitation_rates_and_ BTD_medications_Letter_to_CMS_Nov%2011.pdf.

[65] Tufts Center for the Study of Drug Development, "Cost to Develop and Win Marketing Approval for a New Drug Is $2.6 Billion," November 18, 2014, at http://csdd.tufts.edu/ news/complete_story/pr_tufts_csdd_2014_cost_study.

[66] Christopher Adams and Van Brantner,"Estimating the Cost of New Drug Development. Is it Really $802 Million?" *Health Affairs*, vol. 25, no. 2 (March 2006), pp. 420-428, at http://content.healthaffairs.org/content/25/2/420.long; Donald Light and Rebecca Warburton, "Demythologizing the High Costs of Pharmaceutical Research," *BioSocieties*, London School of Economics, 1-17, 2011, at http://www.pharmamyths.net/files/ Biosocieties_2011_Myths_of_High_Drug_Research_Costs.pdf.

[67] CRS Report R41705, *The National Institutes of Health (NIH): Background and Congressional Issues*, by Judith A. Johnson.

[68] David Austin, *Research and Development in the Pharmaceutical Industry*, Congressional Budget Office, 2006, at http://www.cbo.gov/sites/default/files/cbofiles/ftpdocs/76xx/doc7615/10-02-drugr-d.pdf.

[69] Geoffrey Joyce, Dana Goldman, Pinar Karaca-Mandic and Grant Lawless, "Impact of Specialty Drugs on Use of Other Medical Services," *American Journal of Managed Care*, vol. 14, vo. 12 (December 2008), pp. 821-828, at http://www.ncbi.nlm.nih.gov/pmc/articles/PMC3767569/. The authors suggested that insurers would be better off finding ways to manage utilization so that patients who would benefit from the drugs had access to them, rather than restricting access through high patient cost sharing or formulary requirements designed to deter use by all patients, regardless of clinical need.

[70] Pinar Karaca-Mandic, Jeffrey McCullough, Mustaqeem Siddiqui, Holly Van Houten, and Nilay Shah, "Impact of New Drugs and Biologics on Colorectal Cancer Treatment and Costs," *Journal of Oncology Practice*, vol. 7, no. 3 (May 2011), pp. e30s–e37s, at http://www.ncbi.nlm.nih.gov/pmc/articles/PMC3092464/. David Howard, John Kauh, and Joseph Lipscomb, "The Value of New Chemotherapeutic Agents for Metastatic Colorectal Cancer," *Archives of Internal Medicine*, vol. 170, no. 6 (March 22, 2010); pp.537-542, at http://www.ncbi.nlm.nih.gov/pubmed/20233802/.

[71] Jagpreet Chhatwal, Fasiha Kanwal, Mark Roberts, and Michael Dunn; "Cost-Effectiveness and Budget Impact of Hepatitis C Virus Treatment with Sofosbuvir and Ledipasvir in the United States," *Annals of Internal Medicine*, vol. 162, no. 6 (March 17, 2015), pp. 397-406, at http://annals.org/article.aspx?articleid=2197176.

[72] Ibid. The study estimated the average discount on drugs given to payers based on the discounts for Sovaldi. According to the study, private, VA, Medicare, and Medicaid discounts were 14%, 44%, 0% and 23%, respectively. By then adjusting for the number of patients under each insurance type, the study estimated the average discount was 11%. The authors used projections of expected quality-adjusted life-years, total lifetime costs, and cost of antiviral drugs to estimate the incremental cost-effectiveness of new drugs compared with previous treatments. See the study for more information.

[73] See "Sovaldi as Case Study of Payer Negotiations."

[74] David Howard, Peter Bach, Ernst Berndt, and Rena Conti,"Pricing in the Market for Anticancer Drugs," *Journal of Economic Perspectives*, vol. 29, no. 1(Winter 2015), pp. 139–162, at http://pubs.aeaweb.org/doi/pdfplus/10.1257/jep.29.1.139.

[75] Institute for Clinical and Economic Review, "Emerging Therapy Assessment and Pricing," at http://www.icerreview.org/etap/.

[76] About 20% of insured consumers are now enrolled in high-deductible health plans (HDHP) that have lower premiums and higher deductibles than traditional insurance plans. Some HDHPs cover preventive care, including vaccinations and certain drugs, before an enrollee has met the plan deductible. In other HDHP plans, employees must cover prescription costs out-of-pocket until they reach a set-dollar deductible. According to America's Health Insurance Plans (AHIP), there were nearly 17.4 million enrollees in HDHPs in January 2014, up from 11.4 million in January 2011. (AHIP, "New Census Survey Shows Increased Growth in HSA Enrollment," July 9, 2014, at https://www.ahip.org/Press-Room/2014/HSA-Census-Survey/.) HDHP enrollees may pay for drugs and other services with tax-advantaged health savings accounts or may have access to other, employer-provided health reimbursement. See CRS Report RS21573, *Tax-Advantaged Accounts for Health Care Expenses: Side-by-Side Comparison, 2013*, by Carol Rapaport. Some health insurance plans

sold on state exchanges impose deductibles for prescription drugs or include prescription drugs in their overall deductibles. Average prescription-drug-only deductibles ranged from $134 to $465 in 2015. Kaiser Family Foundation, "Medical and Prescription Drug Deductibles for Plans Offered in Federally Facilitated and Partnership Marketplaces for 2015," November 18, 2014, at http://kff.org/health-reform/fact-sheet/medical-and-prescription-drug-deductibles-for-plans-offered-in-federally-facilitated-and-partnership-marketplaces-for2015/.

[77] Walgreens/Pharmacy Benefit Management Institute, *2014 PBMI Specialty Drug Benefit Report*, at http://reports.pbmi.com/report.php?id=5. (Registration required.) The report is based on responses from 306 U.S. employers, health plans, and other plan sponsors representing 17.6 million covered lives.

[78] The FDA defines a brand-name drug as a drug marketed under a proprietary, trademark-protected name.

[79] Kaiser Family Foundation, *2014 Employer Health Benefits Survey, Section Nine: Prescription Drug Benefits*, September 10, 2014, at http://kff.org/report-section/ehbs-2014-section-nine-prescription-drug-benefits/.

[80] Stephanie Regnier, "How Does Drug Coverage Vary by Insurance Type? Analysis of Drug Formularies in the United States," *The American Journal of Managed Care*, April 21, 2014, at http://www.ajmc.com/publications/issue/2014/2014-vol20-n4/how-does-drug-coverage-vary-by-insurance-type-analysis-of-drug-formularies-in-the-united-states.

[81] Kaiser Family Foundation, *2014 Employer Health Benefits Survey, Section Nine: Prescription Drug Benefits*, September 10, 2014, at http://kff.org/report-section/ehbs-2014-section-nine-prescription-drug-benefits/.

[82] Kaiser Family Foundation, *2014 Employer Health Benefits Survey, Section Nine,* Exhibit 9.4, at http://kff.org/reportsection/ehbs-2014-section-nine-prescription-drug-benefits/. There also was wider pricing for insurers requiring coinsurance. Shelly Carrey, Pharmacy Benefit Management Institute, "8 Ways Pharmacy Benefit Design May Evolve in 2013," The Institute for Health Care Consumerism, at http://www.theihcc.com/en/communities/pharmacy_benefit_management/8-ways-pharmacy-benefit-design-may-evolve-in-2013_hfpq9mpi.html.

[83] CRS Report R42069, *Private Health Insurance Market Reforms in the Affordable Care Act (ACA)*, by Annie L. Mach and Bernadette Fernandez. On average, Bronze plans will cover 60% of a base benefit package; Silver plans, 70%; Gold plans, 80%; and Platinum plans, 90%. (Qualified health insurance plans must be certified by a state exchange and must provide a minimum level of benefits, although insurers may offer more comprehensive coverage. To receive ACA cost sharing and premium subsidies, consumers must buy qualified plans through an exchange.)

[84] Exchanges are special marketplaces where consumers can buy health plans that meet set federal requirements and also qualify for federal premium subsidies to defray part of the cost of the plans. See CRS Report R42663, *Health Insurance Exchanges Under the Patient Protection and Affordable Care Act (ACA)*, by Bernadette Fernandez and Annie L. Mach.

[85] Avalere, "Exchange Plans Increase Costs of Specialty Drugs for Patients in 2015." Link to study available at Caroline Pearson, Avalere Health, "Consumers Likely Face High Out-Of-Pocket Costs for Specialty Drugs In Exchange Plans," at http://avalerehealth.net/expertise/managed-care/insights/consumers-likely-face-high-out-ofpocket-costs-for-specialty-drugs-in-excha.The study looked at 603 plan designs offered by 60 different carriers in 19 states.

[86] Ibid.

[87] See "Outstanding Issues."

[88] Dana Goldman, Geoffrey Joyce, Yuhui Zheng, "Prescription Drug Cost Sharing: Associations wWith Medication and Medical Utilization and Spending and Health," *Journal of the American Medical Association*, vol. 298, no. 1 (July 4, 2007), at http://jama.jamanetwork.com/article.aspx?articleid=207805.

[89] RAND Health, "Prescription Drug Cost-Sharing: A Powerful Policy Lever to Use with Care," 2009, at http://www.rand.org/content/dam/rand/pubs/research_briefs/2009/RAND_RB9474.pdf; and Dana Goldman, Geoffrey Joyce, Grant Lawless, William Crown, and Vincent Willey, "Benefit Design and Specialty Drug Use," *Health Affairs*, vol. 25, no. 5 (September 2006), pp. 1319-1331, at http://content.healthaffairs.org/content/25/5/1319.full.

[90] Pinar Karaca-Mandic, Geoffrey Joyce, Dana Goldman, and Marianne Laouri, "Cost Sharing, Family Health Care Burden, and the Use of Specialty Drugs for Rheumatoid Arthritis," *Health Service Research*, Oct 2010; vol. 45, no. 5, part I (October 2010), pp. 1227–1250, at http://www.ncbi.nlm.nih.gov/pmc/articles/PMC2965502/.

[91] Catherine Starner, G. Caleb Alexander, Kevin Bowen, Yang Qiu, Peter Wickersham, and Patrick Gleason, "Specialty Drug Coupons Lower Out-Of-Pocket Costs And May Improve Adherence At The Risk Of Increasing Premiums," *Health Affairs*, vol. 33, no. 10 (October 2014), pp. 1761-1769, at http://content.healthaffairs.org/content/33/10/1761.abstract.

[92] Andrew Pollack, "Health Insurers Pressing Down on Drug Prices," *The New York Times*, June 20, 2014, at http://www.nytimes.com/2014/06/21/business/health-plans-bring-pressure-to-bear-on-drug-prices.html.

[93] §1128B(b) of the Social Security Act. For background see CRS WSLG246, Earning Rewards when Buying Drugs Covered by Medicare and Medicaid: HHS Gives the Green Light, by Jennifer A. Staman.

[94] Artemetrx, *Specialty Drug Trend Across the Pharmacy and Medical Benefit*, 2013, p. 2, at http://www.artemetrx.com/docs/ARTEMETRX_Specialty_Trend_Rpt.pdf; and Prime Therapeutics, "Specialty Drugs are Forecasted to be 50% of All Drug Expenditures in 2018," at http://cdn2.content.compendiumblog.com/uploads/user/e7c690e8-6ff9-102a-ac6d-e4aebca50425/accf0d87-0d14-4aa7-bbf3-193b90c8d68c/File/1f8476cb4a60eb4728 93ddf381c9c3ec/prediction_that_by_2018__more_than_50_percent_of_all_drug_ expenditures_will_be_specialty.pdf.

[95] See "Understanding Specialty Pharmacy Management and Cost Control," Pharmaceutical Strategies Group, June 2010; and Peter Wehrwein,"Should Specialty Drugs Be Shifted From the Medical to Pharmacy Benefit?" *Managed Care*, January 2015, at http://www.managedcaremag.com/archives/2015/1/should-specialty-drugs-be-shifted-medical-pharmacy-benefit. Specialty drug spending estimates can vary depending on whether analysts include drugs purchased under both the pharmacy and medical benefit.

[96] Brenda Motheral and Corey Belkin, "An Evaluation of Specialty Drug Pricing Under the Pharmacy and Medical Benefit," Artemetrx Specialty Drug Solutions, March 2014.

[97] Ibid.

[98] Jordan Shapiro, "Missouri Governor Signs Oral Chemotherapy Bill," *Associated Press*, March 19, 2014, at http://www.newstribune.com/news/2014/mar/19/missouri-governor-signs-oral-chemotherapy-bill/; and Compass Health Analytics, "Actuarial Assessment of the Report of the Committee to Evaluate the Parity between Oral and Intravenous Chemotherapy," prepared for the State of New Hampshire Insurance Department, August 9, 2012, at http://www.nh.gov/insurance/reports/documents/nhid_oralchemoanalysis2012.pdf.

[99] The URAC, formerly known as the Utilization Review Accreditation Commission, and the Accreditation Commission for Health Care (ACHC) are organizations accrediting specialty pharmacies. See https://www.urac.org/about-urac/about-urac/.

[100] Katie Thomas and Andrew Pollack, "Specialty Pharmacies Proliferate, Along with Questions," *The New York Times*, July 15, 2015, at http://www.nytimes.com/2015/07/16/ business/specialty-pharmacies-proliferate-along-withquestions.html?ref=us&_r=0. There are questions about whether PBMs that own specialty pharmacies and make money dispensing the drugs face potential conflicts of interest.

[101] "Catamaran Makes Formulary Cuts, But Preserves Specialty Access," *Drug Benefit News*, vol. 15, no. 13 (July 11, 2014), at http://aishealth.com/sites/all/files/marketplace_pdf_ samples/sampledbn.pdf.

[102] See "Sovaldi as Case Study of Payer Negotiations."

[103] Innovator drugs include single-source products (typically brand-name products that have no available generic versions) and innovator multiple-source products (typically brand-name drugs that have available generic versions).

[104] Medicaid.gov, "Medicaid Drug Rebate Program," at http://www.medicaid.gov/Medicaid-CHIP-ProgramInformation/By-Topics/Benefits/Prescription-Drugs/Medicaid-Drug-Rebate-Program.html.

[105] CRS Report CRS Report R43778, *Medicaid Prescription Drug Pricing and Policy*, by Cliff Binder.

[106] Government Accountability Office, *Prescription Drugs: Comparison of DOD and VA Direct Purchase Prices*, April 2013, at http://www.gao.gov/assets/660/654019.pdf.

[107] CRS Report R40611, *Medicare Part D Prescription Drug Benefit*, by Suzanne M. Kirchhoff and Patricia A. Davis.

[108] Ibid. Beneficiaries also receive coverage for drugs under Medicare Part B, which covers certain drugs furnished in a doctor's office or as part of a medical service, and drugs that usually are not self-administered, such as drugs given by infusion or injection. Generally, Medicare reimburses physicians and other providers, such as hospital outpatient clinics, for covered Part B drugs and biologics at 106% of a drug manufacturer's average sales price. Health care providers also are paid separately for administering Medicare Part B drugs. Medicare pays 80% of the amount paid to providers, and beneficiaries are responsible for the remaining 20%. See CRS Report R40425, *Medicare Primer*, coordinated by Patricia A. Davis and Scott R. Talaga.

[109] Panos Kanavos, Alessandra Ferrario, Sotiris Vandoros, and Gerard Anderson, "Higher U.S. Branded Drug Prices and Spending Compared to Other Countries May Stem Partly from Quick Uptake of New Drugs," *Health Affairs*, vol. 32, no. 4 (April 2013), pp. 753-761.

[110] Gilead, "U.S. Food and Drug Administration Approves Gilead's Sovaldi (Sofosbuvir) for the Treatment of Chronic Hepatitis C," December 6, 2013, at http://www.gilead.com/news/ press-releases/2013/12/us-food-and-drugadministration-approves-gileads-sovaldi-sofosbuvir-for-the-treatment-of-chronic-hepatitis-c. The cost of the treatment can be higher if Sovaldi is used in conjunction with other hepatitis C drugs.

[111] Centers for Disease Control, "Hepatitis C FAQs for the Public," at http://www.cdc. gov/hepatitis/c/cfaq.htm.

[112] California Technology Assessment Forum, *The Comparative Clinical Effectiveness and Value of Simeprevir and Sofosbuvir in the Treatment of Chronic Hepatitis C Infection*, Final Report, April 15, 2014, at http://ctaf.org/sites/default/files/assessments/CTAF_Hep_C_ Apr14_final.pdf; and Jagpreet Chhatwal, Fasiha Kanwal, Mark Roberts, and Michael Dunn, "Cost-Effectiveness and Budget Impact of Hepatitis C Virus Treatment With Sofosbuvir and Ledipasvir in the United States," *Annals of Internal Medicine*, vol. 162, no. 6 (March 17, 2015), pp. 397-406, at http://annals.org/article.aspx?articleid=2197176.

[113] Viohl and Associates for the Medicaid Health Plans of America, "The Sovaldi® Squeeze: High Costs Force Tough State Decisions," September 29, 2014, at www.mhpa.org/_upload/SovaldiSqueeze-Oct2014.pdf.

[114] Ibid.

[115] Gilead, "Support Path for Sovaldi and Harvoni," at http://www.gilead.com/responsibility/us-patient-access/support%20path%20for%20sovaldi%20and%20harvoni.

[116] Seeking Alpha, "Gilead Sciences' (GILD) CEO John Martin on Q4 2014 Results – Earnings Call Transcript," February 3, 2015, at http://seekingalpha.com/article/2880996-gilead-sciences-gild-ceo-john-martin-on-q4-2014-resultsearnings-call-transcript.

[117] Ed Silverman, "Ooh La La: France Negotiates a Steep Discount for Sovaldi From Gilead," *Wall Street Journal*, November 20, 2014, at http://blogs.wsj.com/pharmalot/2014/11/20/ooh-la-la-france-negotiates-a-steep-discount-forsovaldi/.

[118] FDA, "FDA Approves First Combination Pill to Treat Hepatitis C," press release, October 10, 2014, at http://www.fda.gov/NewsEvents/Newsroom/PressAnnouncements/ucm418365.htm.

[119] FDA, "FDA Approves Viekira Pak to Treat Hepatitis C," press release, December 19, 2014, at http://www.fda.gov/NewsEvents/Newsroom/PressAnnouncements/ucm427530.htm.

[120] Andrew Pollack, "AbbVie Deal Heralds Changed Landscape for Hepatitis Drugs," *New York Times*, December 22, 2014, at http://www.nytimes.com/2014/12/22/business/pharmacy-deal-heralds-changed-landscape-for-hepatitisdrugs.html and PR Newswire, "Express Scripts and AbbVie Make Hepatitis C Cure Available to Millions of Patients in Need," December 22, 2014, http://www.prnewswire.com/news-releases/express-scripts-and-abbvie-make-hepatitis-ccure-available-to-millions-of-patients-in-need-300012889.html.

[121] Seeking Alpha, "Gilead Sciences' (GILD) CEO John Martin on Q4 2014 Results – Earnings Call Transcript," February 3, 2015, at http://seekingalpha.com/article/2880996-gilead-sciences-gild-ceo-john-martin-on-q4-2014-resultsearnings-call-transcript.

[122] Erin Allday, "Kaiser Reverses Plan to Sharply Boost Patient Cost of HIV Drugs," *SFGate*, February 20, 2015, at http://www.sfgate.com/health/article/Kaiser-reverses-plan-to-sharply-boost-patient-6092204.php.

[123] IMS Health, *Medicine and the Shifting Costs of Healthcare*, April 2014.

[124] Ibid. Many health plans cap annual out-of-pocket spending, but the high co-payments still can be a major burden for consumers who must pay thousands of dollars for their drugs in a matter of months or weeks (or if low income even smaller amounts are more burdensome). While participants in private insurance plans may qualify for manufacturer coupons that reduce cost sharing, pharmaceutical companies may be liable under federal anti-kickback statutes if they offer coupons to induce consumers to buy prescription drugs under federal programs, such as Medicare Part D.

[125] "NHeLP and The AIDS Institute File HIV/AIDS Discrimination Complaint against Florida Health Insurers," press release, May 29, 2014, at http://www.theaidsinstitute.org/sites/default/files/attachments/NHeLP_and_The_AIDS_Institute_File_Civil_Rights_Complaint_Against_Florida_Health_Insurers_FINAL.pdf.

[126] Nicholas Nehmas," Cigna Agrees to Reduce Cost of HIV/AIDS Drugs," *Miami Herald*, November 7, 2014, at http://www.miamiherald.com/news/local/community/miami-dade/article3622324.html.

[127] Douglas Jacobs and Benjamin Sommers "Using Drugs to Discriminate—Adverse Selection in the Insurance Marketplace," *The New England Journal of Medicine*, vol. 372 January 28, 2015, pp. 399-402, at http://www.nejm.org/doi/full/10.1056/NEJMp1411376.

[128] The rules affect individual and fully insured small-group plans regulated by the ACA.

[129] CMS, "Patient Protection and Affordable Care Act; HHS Notice of Benefit and Payment Parameters for 2016," February 20, 2015, at http://www.cms.gov/CCIIO/Resources/Regulations-and-Guidance/.

[130] Policy and Medicine, "Massachusetts Introduces Drug Cost Transparency Bill That Would Cap Prices For Certain Products; North Carolina and Pennsylvania Also Introduce Bills Requiring Drug Cost Reports," April 23, 2015, at http://www.policymed.com/2015/04/massachusetts-introduces-drug-cost-transparency-bill-that-could-cap-prices-forcertain-products-nort.html; and Caitlin Owens, "How States are Working to Control Prescription Drug Costs," *National Journal*, June 1, 2015; and George Lauer, "Drug Price Transparency Bill Shelved in California, Push Continues," *California Healthline*, May 7, 2015, at http://www.californiahealthline.org/insight/2015/drug-price-transparency-billshelved-in-california-push-continues.

[131] Legislation from the 114th Congress includes H.R. 1600, S. 1488, and S. 1566.

[132] Examples include Chapter 536, Laws of New York 2010; Vermont Act 171. Chad Brooker, "Waging War on Specialty Pharmaceutical Tiering in Pharmacy Benefit Design," American University, *Health Law and Policy Brief*, vol 7, no. 2 (2013), pp. 25-48, at http://digitalcommons.wcl.american.edu/cgi/viewcontent.cgi?article=1128&context=hlp.

[133] Maryland House Bill 761. The law defines a specialty drug as a prescription drug prescribed for an individual with a complex or chronic medical condition; that costs $600 or more for a 30-day supply; is not typically stocked at retail pharmacies; and requires difficult or unusual process of delivery to the patient or enhanced patient education, management, or support beyond those required for traditional dispensing before or after administration of the drug.

[134] Ha Tu, Divya Samuel, "Limited Options to Manage Specialty Drug Spending," Center for Studying Health System Change, *HSC Research Brief*, no. 22, April 2012, at http://www.hschange.org/CONTENT/1286/?words=specialty%20drugs.

[135] CRS Report R43934, *President's FY2016 Budget: Centers for Medicare & Medicaid Services (CMS) Legislative Proposals*, coordinated by Alison Mitchell, Kirstin B. Blom, and Patricia A. Davis.

[136] IMS, *Harbingers of Change in Healthcare: Implications for the Role and Use of Medicines*, September 2014, p. 11, at http://www.imshealth.com/vgn-ext-templating/v/index.jsp?vgnextoid=af47009812568410VgnVCM10000076192ca2RCRD.

[137] American Society of Clinical Oncology Value Care Task Force, "Value in Cancer Care," at http://www.asco.org/practice-research/value-cancer-care.

[138] IMS Institute for Health Care Informatics, "How Much Should Drugs Cost? A Big Data Solution," *Forbes* Healthcare Conference, December 3-4, 2014, at http://www.imshealth.com/portal/site/imshealth/menuitem.762a961826aad98f53c753c71ad8c22a/?vgnextoid=a2ce4596eb11a410VgnVCM10000076192ca2RCRD.

[139] Bijal Nitin Patel and Patricia R. Audet, "A Review of Approaches for the Management of Specialty Pharmaceuticals in the United States, " *PharmacoEconomics*, August 14, 2014, at http://www.ncbi.nlm.nih.gov/pmc/articles/PMC4209107/.

[140] CRS Report CRS Report RL32858, *Health Information Technology: Promoting Electronic Connectivity in Healthcare*, by C. Stephen Redhead.

[141] Alessandra Ferrario and Panos Kanavos, London School of Economics and Political Science, *Managed Entry Agreements for Pharmaceuticals: The European Experience*, April 2013. Report prepared under contract to European Commission; and Kari Ruggeri and Ellen Nolte, *Pharmaceutical Pricing, the Use of External Reference Pricing*, RAND Europe, 2013, at http://www.rand.org/content/dam/rand/pubs/research_reports/RR200/RR240/RAND_RR240.pdf.

In: Pharmaceutical Industry Developments
Editor: Kristy Bishop
ISBN: 978-1-63484-649-3

Chapter 2

PRESCRIPTION DRUG DISCOUNT COUPONS: IMPLICATIONS FOR PUBLIC AND COMMERCIAL HEALTH CARE PLANS*

Suzanne M. Kirchhoff

SUMMARY

U.S. pharmaceutical manufacturers offer co-payment coupons to consumers with health insurance to help defray the cost of prescription drugs. Drugmakers offer the coupons on corporate websites, in physician offices, and through television and other media to create a market for a newly introduced drug, to increase the likelihood that a patient will continue an existing prescription, or to bolster the market for brand-name drugs that have lost patent exclusivity and face competition from lower-priced generic substitutes. Coupons can be especially important to individuals who have been prescribed expensive specialty drugs to treat cancer, hepatitis C, and other serious conditions.

The number of pharmaceutical coupon offers has increased in recent years, with manufacturers tendering coupons for more than 500 prescription drugs in 2014, compared with fewer than 100 in 2011. According to one study, coupons were used for about 8% of brand-name prescriptions in 2014, up from 3% in 2011. While manufacturer coupons

---

* This is an edited, reformatted and augmented version of a Congressional Research Service publication R44264, prepared for Members and Committees of Congress, dated November 5, 2015.

may reduce or eliminate a consumer's out-of-pocket spending requirement, generally they do not reduce the price an insurer or government program is charged for a drug. Health care payers, such as commercial insurers, unions and employers, and government programs, say that coupons can actually increase their costs if enrollees use them to buy more expensive brand-name drugs when cheaper generics or other substitute drugs are available.

In addition to offering coupons, manufacturers and charitable organizations run pharmaceutical assistance programs that provide free drugs and other aid to consumers who may not have insurance or are unable to afford a prescribed drug. Retail drugstores and other businesses also offer their own discount cards and customer-incentive programs to increase demand.

Coupon use is prohibited in conjunction with federal health programs such as the Medicare Part D prescription drug benefit. Federal statutes, including antikickback law (Section 1128B (b) of the Social Security Act), prohibit the knowing and willful offer or payment of remuneration to induce a person to buy an item or service that will be reimbursed by a federal health care program. Manufacturers may be liable under the antikickback statute if they offer coupons to induce consumers to purchase drugs under federal programs. In a September 2014 audit, the Department of Health and Human Services' Office of Inspector General found that manufacturers did not have consistent controls in place to prevent Medicare enrollees from using prescription drug coupons in conjunction with their Part D benefits.

In the private sector, some payers have begun to bar enrollees from redeeming coupons for certain prescription products or have chosen not to cover certain drugs that qualify for coupon discounts. Others allow or encourage enrollees to redeem coupons for expensive specialty drugs to improve the odds that the enrollees will complete a prescribed treatment. Studies have shown that enrollees are less likely to adhere to a full course of medication when out-of-pocket payments increase.

INTRODUCTION

Many U.S. pharmaceutical manufacturers offer co-payment coupons, or cards, to defray the consumer cost of prescription drugs. Coupons are designed to reduce or eliminate out-of-pocket payments for insured consumers, such as mandatory prescription co-payments or coinsurance.[1] Many co-payment coupons are targeted at people with chronic conditions and can be particularly important in helping consumers afford new, expensive specialty drugs[2] that are used to treat conditions such as cancer, hepatitis C, and other serious ailments.

A recent study of retail pharmacy data found that enrollees in commercial insurance plans used co-payment coupons for about 8% of brand-name[3] drug prescriptions in 2014, up from 3% in 2011.[4] Some high-cost drugs, including those for multiple sclerosis and rheumatoid arthritis, had 70% coupon usage. Manufacturers also commonly use coupons to support sales of drugs that are not included on insurance plan formularies, or lists of covered drugs.

Pharmaceutical manufacturers, which spend billions of dollars annually on coupons,[5] see co-payment assistance as a necessary response to cost-control strategies by health care payers[6] that can impose large enrollee out-of-pocket payments for some pharmaceuticals, thereby affecting volume and drug pricing.[7] (See "Tiered Pricing.") In addition, studies have found that consumers are less likely to initiate or complete a prescribed course of medication as cost-sharing increases, which can affect overall health outcomes.[8]

Health care payers say that co-payment coupons can provide an incentive for consumers to select more expensive drugs even when cheaper substitutes are available. Although the coupons reduce consumer payments, they do not reduce the price of the drug to health payers. For that reason, coupon redemptions can increase spending by commercial and government payers.[9] More broadly, when consumers are relieved of co-payment obligations, there may be less market constraint on overall drug prices.[10]

There are restrictions on coupon use. The federal antikickback law[11] (Section 1128B (b) of the Social Security Act) prohibits the knowing and willful offer or payment of remuneration to induce a person to buy an item or service that will be reimbursed by a federal health care program. Pharmaceutical manufacturers may be in violation of the antikickback statute if they offer coupons to induce consumers to purchase drugs under federal programs, such as the voluntary Medicare Part D prescription drug program (Medicare Prescription Drug, Improvement, and Modernization Act of 2003, or MMA; P.L. 108-173).[12] (See "Restrictions on Coupon Use.")

In the private sector, some payers and pharmacy benefit managers (PBMs)[13] have barred enrollees from redeeming coupons for certain drugs. Others have decided not to include specific drugs that are eligible for coupon discounts on their formularies.[14]

This report will provide an overview of prescription drug use and payment; explain the difference between coupons and other pharmaceutical assistance and incentive programs offered by manufacturers, pharmacies, states, and nonprofit organizations; and outline federal laws and regulations and private-sector policies relating to coupons and other financial incentives for consumers/patients to purchase prescription drugs.

Common Insurance Terms

Co-payment: A fixed dollar amount that an enrollee in a health care plan pays for a product or service covered by the plan. For example, an insurer may charge a $20 co-payment for a physician visit or a $5 co-payment for a prescription drug.

Coinsurance: The percentage share that an enrollee in a health insurance plan pays for a product or service covered by the plan. For example, an insurer may charge 10% coinsurance for a $100 prescription drug, meaning the consumer's out-of-pocket cost is $10.

Deductible: The amount an enrollee is required to pay for health care services or products before his or her insurance plan begins to provide coverage. An enrollee in an insurance plan with a $500 deductible would be responsible for paying for the first $500 in health care services. In some insurance plans, the deductible does not apply to certain services, such as preventive care. Insurance plans vary regarding whether beneficiaries must meet a deductible for prescription drug coverage.

Formulary: A list of prescription drugs covered by an insurance plan. In an effort to control costs, insurers are imposing what are known as *tight formularies,* which include a more limited number of drugs than traditional formularies. Insurers also are using *tiered formularies*, under which patients are charged lower co-payments or coinsurance for less expensive generic drugs and certain brand-name drugs that are designated by the plan as preferred drugs because they are lower cost or deemed by an insurer to be safer or more effective. Under these tiered formularies, patients are charged higher co-payments or coinsurance for more expensive drugs or drugs that the plan deems to be less effective.

Out-of-Pocket Costs: The total amount an insured consumer pays each year for covered health care services that are not reimbursed by an insurance plan. Out-of-pocket costs can include deductibles, co-payments, and coinsurance.

Out-of-Pocket Maximum: The maximum amount an enrollee must pay before his or her health insurance plan covers 100% of health benefits. Certain costs, such as premiums, generally are not counted toward an out-of-pocket maximum, or cap.

Pharmacy Network: A group of retail, mail-order, and specialty pharmacies that contract with health insurers to dispense covered drugs at a set price. Network pharmacies also may provide other services under contract, such as monitoring patient adherence to drugs.

Pharmacy Benefit Managers (PBMs): Intermediaries between insurers and manufacturers that carry out functions such as designing drug formularies; negotiating prices; creating price tiers and other utilization controls; and administering prescription drug payment systems for health plans, pharmacies, and manufacturers.

Premium: The amount an enrollee pays for health insurance coverage. Many plans charge monthly premiums, but premiums also can be assessed on a quarterly or annual basis.

U.S. SPENDING FOR PRESCRIPTION DRUGS

U.S. prescription drug use has grown substantially during the past several decades as researchers have developed groundbreaking therapies, the number of consumers with prescription drug coverage has expanded, and pharmaceutical companies have increased advertising and other marketing efforts.[15] Reflecting these changes, prescription drugs accounted for about 10% of U.S. health care spending in 2014, up from about 5.5% in 1990.[16]

As recently as 1990, consumers accounted for the bulk of prescription drug spending. Consumer out-of-pocket spending—which includes insurance deductibles and coinsurance or co-payments for filled prescriptions[17]—was 57% of U.S. prescription spending in 1990, whereas commercial payers and taxpayer-financed health programs accounted for about 43%.[18] (See *Figure 1.*)

In the ensuing decades, government health care programs, such as Medicare and Medicaid, expanded prescription drug coverage to tens of millions of consumers.[19] Congress was spurred by rising drug prices, as prescription drug inflation rose faster than inflation for other medical services in the 1990s and early 2000s. The higher prices posed a financial burden for groups such as the uninsured elderly and lower-income consumers.[20] In addition, a larger share of insurance now comes through commercial managed-care plans, which generally impose lower out-of-pocket costs for drugs than other insurance products.[21]

Reflecting these changes in payer mix and policies, consumer out-of-pocket spending is forecast to make up only 16% of prescription drug expenditures in 2014, with private and public health programs covering 84%.[22]

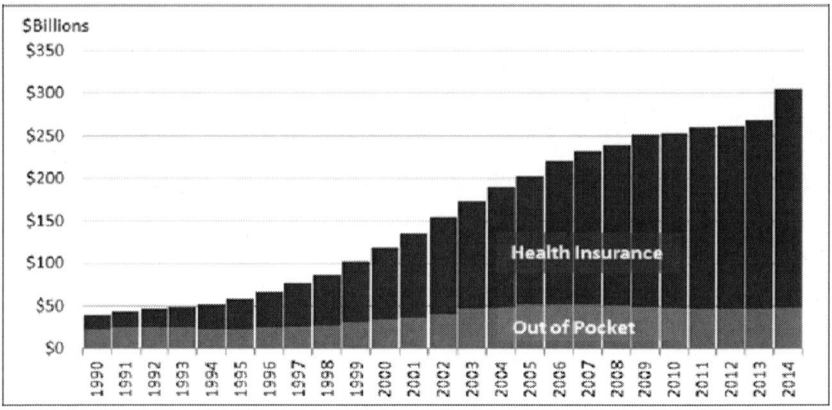

Source: Centers for Medicaid & Medicare Services, National Health Expenditures Data.

Note: Health Insurance includes commercial plans and government programs such as Medicare and Medicaid.

Figure 1. Consumer Out-of-Pocket Spending for Prescription Drugs.

Although out-of-pocket spending has declined as a share of overall drug spending, consumer out-of-pocket spending rose from $23 billion in 1990 to $48 billion in 2014 and is expected to grow to $70 billion by 2024, according to government estimates.[23]

There is also a great deal of variability in out-of-pocket spending among insured individuals depending on the specific drugs they are prescribed and the structure of their health plans. For example, in 2014, only about 20% of brand-name prescriptions filled by consumers across different types of commercial plans had co-payments of $50 or more, according to a study of retail data. However, consumers enrolled in high-deductible health plans (HDHP)[24] were more likely to face co-payments of $50 or more, including about 25% of HDHP claims for brand-name drugs with co-payments of $100 or above.[25]

INSURER PRESCRIPTION DRUG COST CONTROLS

Health care payers use a number of strategies to manage and monitor enrollee pharmaceutical use. Some programs are designed to assist patients with chronic or complex conditions who may be using a number of drugs and are at risk for adverse drug interactions or other health issues.

Other strategies are more focused on containing costs by steering patients toward less expensive pharmaceuticals, when available.

Cost-control efforts have intensified in recent years as more high-priced specialty drugs have come to the market. Specialty medications now account for about a third of U.S. prescription drug spending, and some analysts predict that specialty drugs could make up as much as one-half of total drug spending by 2018.[26] In 2014, U.S. prescription drug spending rose by 12.6% from the previous year—the fastest rate since 2001—led by a 26.5% increase in spending on specialty drugs, according to industry and government data.[27]

Following are some prescription drug cost-management techniques employed by health payers. Even though consumers may face high cost sharing for certain prescriptions, many are enrolled in health care plans that have an overall limit on the amount that enrolled consumers must pay out of pocket for prescription drugs and other health care services during the course of a year. (See text box entitled "Out-of-Pocket Spending Limits," below.)

Deductible

A *deductible* is the amount an insured consumer must pay for covered services before his or her health plan begins to provide reimbursement. If a plan has a $500 deductible, for example, an enrollee would be required to cover expenses up to $500, at which point the plan would begin to pay its share.

An increasing share of the insured population is enrolled in HDHPs, which have higher deductibles than traditional health care plans. HDHPs often are paired with tax-exempt health savings accounts (HSAs) that enrollees can use to pay for qualified medical expenses, such as prescription drugs.[28] Some HDHPs may cover certain prescription drugs as a preventive service without cost sharing, while others may require enrollees to cover prescription costs through an HSA or another spending source until the costs reach a set limit. Some studies have found that enrollees in HDHPs may reduce drug utilization, even in plans where pharmaceuticals are exempt from the deductible.[29]

Many insurance plans sold on state health exchanges established by the Patient Protection and Affordable Care Act (ACA; P.L. 111-148, as amended) impose prescription drug deductibles. An analysis of select ACA plans with prescription drug deductibles found that average annual drug deductibles ranged from $465 for the least generous plans offered to $134 for the most comprehensive products.[30] In general, enrollees in plans with drug deductibles appear to be less likely to adhere to prescriptions than those in plans without such coverage restrictions, and the differences are greater when out-of-pocket costs exceed $50.[31]

After a deductible has been met, health insurance plans may impose co-payments or coinsurance for filled prescriptions. (See "Tiered Pricing.")

Tiered Pricing

Payers commonly use a strategy known as *tiered pricing* to control drug costs and access. In a tiered system, payers impose different co-payments or coinsurance for prescription drugs based on the drug's price, the insurer's assessment of the drug's effectiveness, and the availability of substitute therapies.[32] Payers generally impose lower co-payments for generic[33] or preferred brand-name drugs (i.e., they place the drugs on a lower cost tier), whereas they place drugs that are more expensive or deemed less effective on tiers with higher co-payments or coinsurance.[34] (See *Figure 2*) For example, a generic drug may carry a minimal or zero co-payment, while an enrollee may face 30% coinsurance or more for an expensive specialty drug.

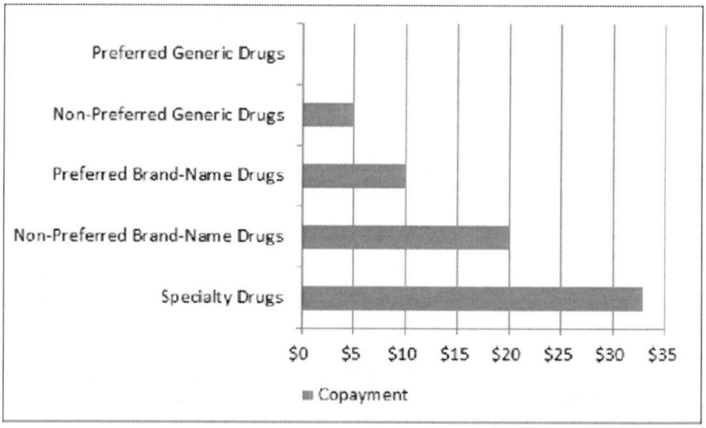

Source: Congressional Research Service.

Notes: For purposes of this graphic, the preferred generic tier has a $0 co-payment, non-preferred generics have a $5 co-payment, preferred brand names have a $10 co-payment, non-preferred brand names have a $20 co-payment, and specialty drugs have 33% coinsurance.

Figure 2. Tiered Formulary (illustrative example of pricing under a tiered formulary for a drug with a $100 price tag).

In 2014, 80% of consumers with employer-sponsored insurance were enrolled in plans that had three or more prescription drug tiers and 20% of consumers were in plans with four or more tiers.[35] Price tiers are used in government health care programs as well. Private insurers that offer Medicare Part D are allowed to place drugs with a negotiated price of more than $600 per month on a specialty tier, with up to 33% coinsurance.[36] Specialty tier drugs made up 0.25% of prescriptions filled by Part D enrollees in 2013 but more than 11% of total Part D drug spending.

There has been a gradual increase in the use of tiered pricing and in the practice of imposing coinsurance, as opposed to flat co-payments, for more expensive drugs. The differential between price tiers has widened over time, imposing a greater financial burden on consumers who use higher-priced drugs.[37] In 2000, a two- or three-tier design was most common in commercial insurance plans, with an average $8 co-payment for a tier-one drug and an average $29 co-payment for a tier-three product. By 2014, more insurers had moved to plans with a higher-priced fourth tier for specialty drugs. In 2014, the average first-tier co-payment was $11 and the average fourth-tier co-payment was $83.[38]

Not all specialty drugs placed on high cost-sharing tiers have lower-cost equivalents.[39] Further, in some instances, insurers have clustered most or all drugs for treating specific conditions, such as HIV/AIDS, on specialty price tiers.[40] The Centers for Medicare & Medicaid Services (CMS) in February 2015 warned insurers offering health insurance through ACA exchanges that placing most or all drugs to treat a specific condition on the highest cost tiers would "effectively discriminate against, or discourage enrollment by, individuals who have those chronic conditions."[41]

Out-of-Pocket Spending Limits

Most private health insurance plans place an annual cap, or maximum, on enrollee out-of-pocket spending, after which the payer covers all or most of the cost of health care services.[42] For 2015, the ACA limits out-of-pocket spending for non-grandfathered non-group and small-group health insurance sold on and off state health exchanges to $6,600 for non-group and $13,200 for small-group plans. The spending limit includes out-of-pocket payments for prescription drugs. For 2015, Medicare Part D enrollees who incur $4,700 in annual out-of-pocket spending enter the catastrophic portion of the benefit, in which they pay a maximum of 5% coinsurance or a nominal co-payment, whichever is greater.

MANUFACTURER CO-PAYMENT COUPONS

Pharmaceutical firms offer co-payment coupons or cards to consumers to help reduce the out-of-pocket costs of prescription drugs. These coupons may benefit pharmaceutical firms by helping to create demand for newly introduced drugs, increase consumer adherence to existing prescriptions, and bolster the market for brand-name drugs that have lost patent exclusivity and face competition from lower-priced generics or other substitutes.[43]

For a sense of how a coupon works, consider a pharmaceutical manufacturer that sells a brand-name drug to a commercial payer for $1,000 for a 30-day supply.[44] The payer places the drug on a specialty price tier that imposes 25% enrollee coinsurance up to the plan's annual out-of-pocket maximum. To bolster sales of the drug, the manufacturer offers a coupon that limits out-of-pocket costs to $100 per 30-day refill for a 12-month period, up to a maximum subsidy of $2,000. In the absence of the manufacturer coupon, an enrollee would pay $250 out of pocket each time he or she went to a pharmacy to buy a 30-day supply of the drug (25% of the $1,000 price). With a coupon, the consumer would pay $100 per fill and the manufacturer would cover the remaining $150 of the required coinsurance.

Most co-payment coupons include disclaimers stating that they cannot be used by individuals enrolled in federal health programs, including Medicare, Medicaid, and the Veterans Health Administration. (See "Restrictions on Coupon Use.") Manufacturers build the cost of co-payment coupons into their budget and pricing strategies.[45]

Coupon Processing

Coupons come in many forms. They can be printed in a magazine or circular, offered electronically—such as a discount number sent as a text to a smart device—or presented as a debit-type card.[46] Coupons loaded on smartphones can provide automatic reminders to a consumer to refill a prescription. Manufacturers may offer starter cards that patients can use to receive an initial fill of a prescription at no cost while they wait for a coverage decision from their health plan.[47]

When an insured consumer presents a prescription at a pharmacy, the pharmacist uses an electronic routing system[48] to submit a claim to the pharmacy benefit manager (PBM) that manages the consumer's specific pharmacy benefit. The PBM processes the initial drug claim and determines the patient's cost-sharing obligation for the drug. The PBM's electronic processing system then submits secondary claims to other payers. Secondary payments can include a second insurance policy held by the individual or a manufacturer coupon. If a coupon is presented, the PBM system, using special codes, will route a coupon to a manufacturer for payment.[49] After all payments are processed, the consumer covers the remaining co-payment, if any.

In some cases, manufacturer discounts are not processed through the electronic system. Some coupon offers take the form of a rebate or discount after the point of sale. In this case, a consumer may make the required co-payment imposed by his or her primary insurance plan when filling a prescription, then send the pharmacy receipt and rebate offer to the manufacturer to secure the promised discount.[50] Consumers also may use a coupon and pay cash for a drug that is not covered by an insurance plan.

Coupon Distribution and Market Impact

Manufacturers advertise coupons through the media and via direct-mail offers. Consumers can download coupons from manufacturer websites or browse available coupons on special websites that aggregate offers from a variety of drugmakers.[51]

Industry data on co-payment coupon distribution and use are available from manufacturers, consulting firms, PBMs, and various websites that serve as online clearinghouses for coupon offers. According to consulting firm Zitter Health Insights, there were 423 co-payment offset programs in winter 2014, covering 544 brands from 131 manufacturers.[52] The company reported that discount offers for hepatitis C drugs such as Sovaldi under these programs had a maximum yearly benefit of $33,563, reflecting the high price of the specialty products. Cancer drug discount offers under these programs had an average annual benefit of $21,103. Drugs for treating rheumatoid arthritis had the highest number of specialty drug co-payment programs.

A separate analysis of retail pharmacy data found that co-payment coupons or vouchers were used by more than 14 million patients in the 12-month period ending in October 2012, of whom 90% used one program and 10% used multiple programs.[53] Most of the coupons were used by patients with chronic conditions. The range of savings was wide, with coupons reducing costs by $40 on average.

One industry analyst has estimated that manufacturer coupon offers are equal to about 1%-2% of annual retail drug spending. [54] While coupon offers may be for a limited time period, such as six months or one year, they are often renewed by manufacturers, who use them as a means to build loyalty to a brand.[55] Manufacturers may use coupons as part of a marketing strategy to keep prices for brand-name drugs higher than they otherwise would be after a lower-cost generic substitute comes to market. Such a strategy was used when Pfizer blockbuster drug Lipitor was exposed to generic competition, for example.[56] Vendors that work with pharmaceutical companies to distribute pharmaceutical coupons say their internal data show that the programs increase prescription drug adherence and increase the duration of therapy.[57]

In addition, coupon programs can generate data regarding patient income, age, and insurance status that can be used by a company to develop pricing, marketing, and other strategies.[58] For example, companies can use data on differences in patient adherence to drugs in various U.S. geographic regions to target coupon offers and other marketing efforts. Electronic coupons can generate data regarding what drugs physicians prescribe and which patients use them. Companies can correlate the information with other electronic data on consumer shopping patterns.

Physicians

Physicians, who prescribe most of the drugs used in the United States, are a focal point for manufacturers. A number of physicians have questioned the cost-effectiveness of some high-priced medications.[59] At the same time, physicians often search out coupons, samples, or other assistance to help their patients afford needed treatments. (See "Patient Assistance Programs.")

The widespread adoption of electronic health records by physician practices is offering a faster, more efficient way for manufacturers and marketers to reach physicians and their patients. Physicians may now enter a prescription into an electronic system that has been programmed to automatically call up information on co-payment coupon offers[60] and can send the offer to a pharmacy along with the prescription. When the consumer fills the claim, the pharmacy processes the coupon as it fills the prescription.

Web-based platforms and software applications have been developed to help health care professionals locate coupons, distribute samples, or procure other discounts for their patients. In one example, Physicians Interactive and McKesson Patient Relationship Solutions announced Coupons on Demand, a web-based platform that physicians can search to find coupons and other discounts.[61]

Other Drug Discount Coupons

Pharmacies, insurers, and other nonprofit groups may offer their own prescription drug cards or programs. These cards generally cannot be used with government benefits or private insurance. Consumer organizations say that drugstore discount cards can provide valuable benefits but that it can be hard to determine whether consumers are receiving the best price with the coupons given that retail drug prices can vary widely among pharmacies in the same geographic area. [62] Although a card may show the price for a specific drug at participating pharmacies, it may not show the full range of prices at all area pharmacies. Websites such as Good Rx[63] have been created to help consumers comparison shop for prescription drugs.

RESTRICTIONS ON COUPON USE

Federal Programs

Co-payment coupons cannot be used in conjunction with federal health benefits, including Medicare, Medicaid, TRICARE military insurance, and Veterans Health Administration programs. The prohibition is based on the federal antikickback statute,[64] which covers various types of remuneration—including kickbacks, bribes, and rebates—whether made directly or indirectly, overtly or covertly, in cash or in kind.[65] Pharmaceutical companies may be liable under the antikickback statute, for example, if they offer coupons to induce the purchase of drugs paid for by federal health care programs.

Retailers and other entities that submit claims to federal agencies for items or services resulting from a violation of the antikickback statute may also face civil monetary penalties and damages under the False Claims Act.[66] For example, the Kmart corporation paid $1.4 million to resolve allegations that it violated the False Claims Act by using manufacturer drug coupons and gasoline discounts to induce Medicare Part D beneficiaries to use its pharmacies.[67]

Federal Employees Health Benefit Program and ACA Qualified Health Plans

Private health plans sold to federal workers through the Federal Employees Health Benefit (FEHB) Program are not considered government programs. Enrollees in these plans may use drug discount coupons or pharmacy incentive programs in concert with their insurance benefits.[68]

The situation is somewhat less clear regarding individuals who enroll in qualified health plans[69] sold through ACA state exchanges. Former HHS Secretary Kathleen Sebelius in an October 2013 letter to Representative James McDermott[70] and a February 2014 letter to Senator Charles Grassley[71] said the HHS did not consider qualified health plans, as well as tax subsidies and other assistance to ACA consumers, to be federal programs. Some manufacturers and health care analysts were concerned that the letter does not constitute formal policy and asked HHS for clarification. Other manufacturers offer coupons to individuals who sign up for ACA-qualified health plans.

Exceptions to the Federal Coupon Prohibition

In 2013, in response to a request from retailers, the HHS OIG issued an advisory opinion stating that supermarkets that operated in-store or stand-alone pharmacies could provide gasoline discounts to customers who signed up for free store cards. The store cards offered financial rewards based on the amount the customers spent in the store, including spending on items covered by federal health care programs. The OIG found that the arrangements would not be subject to enforcement under the false claims or the antikickback statutes.[72] The HHS OIG in October 2014 proposed rules that would include a safe harbor from the antikickback statute and civil monetary penalty rules for certain retailer reward programs.[73]

Purchases by Enrollees "Outside" a Government Benefit

There may be cases in which an individual covered by a federal health plan goes "outside" his or her federal benefit to purchase prescription drugs. A Medicare Part D beneficiary may decide to pay cash for a drug at a retail pharmacy if doing so is cheaper than buying the drug through his or her Part D plan.

Although a Part D enrollee may use a coupon to purchase a drug outside the program, only the actual price paid for the drug—minus all discounts—counts toward Part D annual out-of-pocket spending limits.[74] Some manufacturers have aimed coupons at Medicare recipients who go outside the benefit. Pfizer has made coupons for Lipitor, a cholesterol-battling drug, available to Part D beneficiaries who agree not to use them in tandem with their Part D benefit.[75]

Pharmacists may be unwilling to redeem coupons for enrollees in federal programs, even if the enrollees pay outside of their benefits, due to concerns about possible violations of federal law.

HHS Office of Inspector General Report

A recent report from the Department of Health and Human Services' Office of Inspector General (HHS OIG) said that pharmaceutical manufacturers did not have consistent, effective safeguards to prevent Medicare Part D beneficiaries from using co-payment coupons along with program benefits.[76]

According to the report, not all manufacturer offers carry a disclaimer stating that the coupons, rebates, or other incentives may not be used by individuals enrolled in federal health care programs or in conjunction with federal benefits. The report noted that manufacturers that redeem coupons through PBM electronic claims systems have set up edits at the point of sale designed to identify individuals who may be enrolled in federal programs such as Medicare. For example, when an enrollee submits a coupon with a prescription, and when it is submitted to a manufacturer as a secondary payer, the manufacturer may check for a patient's primary insurance, Part D benefit stage,[77] and date of birth. (Actual Part D enrollment data is not available from CMS.)

However, the HHS OIG report found that the staged system for processing prescription drug claims can make it difficult for entities other than manufacturers to identify coupons as they move through the pharmacy transaction system. The report also noted that coupons redeemed after the point of sale, such as mail-in rebates, may not be detected by electronic safeguard systems.

HHS issued a special advisory bulletin warning manufacturers that they faced potential penalties if they failed to take appropriate steps to ensure that such coupons do not induce the purchase of federal health care program items or services.[78]

Private Insurance

Commercial payers have varying policies regarding coupon use. A 2014 Pharmacy Benefits Management Institute survey found that some large employers (or the plans they contracted with) limited the ability of employees covered under health plans they offer to redeem coupons on the grounds that the coupons interfered with price tiers and other cost-control strategies. Some large employers increased required coinsurance for drugs if a coupon was available.[79]

In 2012, UnitedHealthcare began to bar enrollees from using co-payment coupons for certain specialty drugs.[80] Express Scripts, the nation's largest PBM, dropped 48 drugs from its preferred formulary in 2014, basing its decision partly on the availability of manufacturer co-payment coupons for the drugs.[81] (Insurers that contract with PBMs are not bound to use the PBMs' drug benefit formularies, though many do.) In announcing its decision, Express Scripts noted that prices for the most commonly used generic medications had decreased by more than 40% during the previous five years, whereas prices for commonly used brand-name drugs had risen by more than 65%—meaning that choosing brand-name drugs over generics was imposing a growing cost on insurance plans.

Some patients and manufacturers get around plan prohibitions by using debit cards and rebate offers after the point of sale. For example, one company uses a case study to market its prescription-drug debit card. The case study notes that a manufacturer risked losing thousands of patients after a payer decided to bar co-payment cards for a rheumatoid arthritis drug and instead recommended that its enrollees use a less expensive generic drug. In response, the manufacturer adopted a debit card system, where patients paid the required co-payment at the pharmacy and were reimbursed after the point of the sale—usually within a few days. The debit card vendor reported that this approach resulted in a high patient retention rate.[82]

Insurer Lawsuits

In 2012, a group of union-based health plans brought lawsuits against eight drug manufacturers, charging that their coupon programs violated federal racketeering and commercial bribery laws. Federal district courts have dismissed several of the lawsuits, which were coordinated by the Prescription Action Litigation Coalition of the nonprofit group Community Catalyst.[83]

FINANCIAL IMPACT OF COUPONS

Health care payers and government officials have complained that drug coupons mask the actual price of drugs and may prompt beneficiaries to choose more expensive drugs, even if cheaper, equally effective drugs are available, which can drive up health care spending.[84] Manufacturers have countered that coupons are targeted primarily at higher-priced drugs for which there are few generic substitutes.[85] By improving adherence, they say, the coupons can help to hold down other associated health care costs, such as hospitalizations.

Studies have sought to quantify the impacts of coupon use on consumer behavior and payer spending. For example, a targeted study of consumers using statins to control cholesterol levels found the use of manufacturer coupons increased enrollee prescription adherence but at the cost of higher out-of-pocket spending for consumers and higher costs to their insurance plans than for those using generic drugs or brand-name drugs that did not offer coupons.[86]

A 2014 *Health Affair*s study using data from Prime Therapeutics, a PBM owned by a group of Blue Cross and Blue Shield plans, found that coupons helped consumers save $6 of every $10 in out-of-pocket costs for specialty drugs, making the high-cost products affordable for more patients and potentially improving adherence. However, the increased use of coupons could increase costs for other beneficiaries in a health care plan if a payer decides to raise plan premiums or deductibles to offset some of the expenses of higher drug utilization.[87]

Other studies have examined whether coupons are targeted at drugs for which lower-cost substitutes are available, thus inducing beneficiaries to use higher-priced drugs. A 2013 study looked at whether coupons were being offered for drugs for which either a generic substitute or a therapeutically equivalent product[88] was available. According to that study, about 60% of the coupons examined were for drugs with lower-cost alternatives in the same drug class.[89]

PATIENT ASSISTANCE PROGRAMS

Pharmaceutical manufacturers, state governments, and nonprofit groups offer additional assistance programs for both insured and uninsured consumers.

Pharmaceutical Patient Assistance Programs

A number of manufacturers and nonprofit groups offer patient assistance programs (PAPs) to help uninsured or underinsured individuals obtain access to drugs.[90] PAPs may provide financial assistance or free or reduced-price drugs. Some PAPs provide aid directly to patients, whereas others work through health care providers, such as clinics or hospitals.[91]

To participate in a PAP, an individual generally fills out an application listing information including income,[92] insurance status, medical background, and proof of U.S. citizenship or legal residence. Applications often must be signed by a patient and a physician. Some PAPs provide drugs free of charge to patients who qualify, whereas others subsidize most of the cost of the products. The pharmaceutical industry operates the Partnership for Prescription Assistance,[93] a clearinghouse for information about more than 475 PAPs. According to the partnership, the pharmaceutical industry has aided 8.5 million U.S. consumers through such programs. Other websites with information about such PAPs include NeedyMeds and RxAssist.

CMS has special data exchanges that coordinate government programs with PAPs, State Pharmaceutical Assistance Programs (SPAPs) (see "State Pharmaceutical Assistance Programs") and AIDS drug assistance programs.[94] CMS operates a webpage where consumers can check to see whether there is a PAP for a particular drug.[95] Some PAPs do not accept applications from individuals who are enrolled in Medicare.[96]

HHS OIG Advisory Opinions

In November 2005, HHS OIG issued a special advisory bulletin regarding the application of federal antikickback and other laws to PAPs that aid Medicare Part D beneficiaries.[97] The OIG recognized that manufacturer-based PAPs that subsidize Part D cost sharing presented heightened risks under the antikickback statute. However, it said that cost-sharing assistance provided by truly independent charities should not raise antikickback concerns, even if the charities received manufacturer donations. The OIG also said manufacturer-based PAPs could operate outside the Part D benefit, meaning that no PAP payment for a covered drug could be filed with a Part D plan and manufacturer assistance would not count toward a beneficiary's Part D out-of-pocket spending totals.[98]

In a follow-up bulletin in May 2014,[99] the HHS OIG expanded on its original guidance and said it would apply increased scrutiny to charitable PAPs that establish or operate disease funds that limit assistance to a subset of available products, such as covering co-payments only for expensive or specialty drugs. The bulletin said the cost of a drug was not an appropriate standalone factor for determining individual financial need and that generous financial support, particularly for a PAP with a limited number of drugs or the drugs of a major donor manufacturer, could be evidence of intent to induce use of that drug rather than to support financially needy patients.

State Pharmaceutical Assistance Programs

SPAPs are financed by states to serve uninsured residents or to fill in the gaps in Medicare, Medicaid, and private insurance coverage. SPAPs are aimed at lower-income individuals and usually are the payer of last resort, meaning the SPAP will pay only after federal government programs or any private insurance has already been billed. SPAP rules and coverage vary by state—some are targeted at seniors; some at specific disease groups such as people with HIV/AIDs. Medicare provides a link to SPAPs by state at http://www.medicare.gov/pharmaceutical-assistance-program/state-programs.aspx.[100]

APPENDIX A. NATIONAL EXPENDITURE DATA

For purposes of the National Health Expenditures prescription drug data:

- *Private insurance* includes employer-sponsored insurance and other private insurance, including plans sold through Patient Protection and Affordable Care Act (ACA; P.L. 111-148, as amended) state marketplaces. Private insurance accounted for about 42.8% of prescription drug spending in 2014.
- *Government health care* includes Medicare and Medicaid, which made up 27.9% and 8.9% of prescription drug spending, respectively, in 2014.
- *Other health insurance programs* include the Children's Health Insurance Program and Department of Defense and Department of Veterans Affairs coverage. These programs made up 3.4% of spending in 2014.

- *Other third-party payers* include worksite health care, other private revenues, Indian Health Service, workers' compensation, general assistance, maternal and child health, vocational rehabilitation, other federal programs, Substance Abuse and Mental Health Services Administration, other state and local programs, and school health. They made up less than 1% of spending in 2014.

The National Health Expenditures data measure retail prescription drug spending and do not capture some pharmacy spending by institutions, such as hospitals and physicians' offices.

APPENDIX B. FEDERAL HEALTH PROGRAMS

Federal Role in Prescription Drug Coverage

Medicare Part D: The Medicare Prescription Drug, Improvement, and Modernization Act of 2003 (MMA; P.L. 108- 173) established a voluntary outpatient prescription drug benefit under Medicare Part D, effective January 1, 2006. Medicare Part D provides coverage through private prescription drug plans (PDPs) that offer only drug coverage, or through Medicare Advantage (MA) prescription drug plans (MA-PDs) that offer coverage as part of broader, managed-care plans. Private drug plans participating in Part D bear some financial risk, though federal subsidies cover most program costs in an effort to encourage participation and keep benefits affordable.[101]

Medicare Part B: Certain specified outpatient prescription drugs are covered under Medicare Part B, including drugs furnished incident to physicians' services, immunosuppressive drugs following a Medicare-covered organ transplant, oral anticancer drugs (provided they have the same active ingredients and are used for the same indications as chemotherapy drugs that would be covered if furnished incident to physicians' services), and drugs used for durable medical equipment. Generally, Medicare reimburses physicians and other providers, such as hospital outpatient clinics, for covered Part B drugs and biologics at 106% of a drug manufacturer's average sales price.[102]

Medicaid: Medicaid is a federal-state entitlement program that pays for health care and related services on behalf of certain low-income individuals. Prescription drugs are an optional Medicaid benefit, and all states cover outpatient drugs. States can create formularies, but federal rules tend to result in comprehensive coverage, even for beneficiaries enrolled in Medicaid managed-care plans. Pharmaceutical manufacturers that voluntarily participate in Medicaid are required to pay rebates to states on covered outpatient drugs, which help Medicaid receive manufacturers' lowest or best price.[103]

Children's Health Insurance Program: The state Children's Health Insurance Program (CHIP) is a federal-state program that provides health coverage to certain uninsured, low-income children and pregnant women in families that have annual income above Medicaid eligibility levels but that have no health insurance. CHIP is jointly financed by the federal government and states. Most CHIP plans cover major medical benefits, such as inpatient and outpatient care, physician services, and prescription drugs.[104]

The Veterans Health Administration (VA): The VA offers all enrolled veterans a standard medical benefits package that includes (among other things) inpatient care, outpatient care, and prescription drugs. Prescription drug benefits include over-the-counter drugs and medical and surgical supplies available under the VA national formulary system. The Department of Defense and the VA use certain federal pricing arrangements for these direct purchases, including Federal Supply Schedule prices and prices available to the four largest federal purchasers.[105]

ACA Exchange Plans: The ACA requires that U.S. health care plans offered in the non-group and small-group markets cover at least 10 essential health benefits (EHB), including prescription drugs. Although the ACA imposed minimum standards for the drug benefit, recent studies have found significant differences in the cost and scope of drug coverage among health plans. The Centers for Medicare & Medicaid Services in February 2015 announced more stringent rules for the EHB drug benefit and warned insurers that imposing high cost sharing for most or all medications used to treat a specific disease could constitute discrimination.[106]

End Notes

[1] See text box entitled "Common Insurance Terms," below.

[2] There is no set definition of specialty drugs, although insurers and other health care payers often characterize them as expensive prescription products requiring extra handling or administration that are used to treat complex diseases. Biologics, or drugs derived from living cells, are often specialty drugs. See CRS Report R44132, Specialty Drugs: Background and Policy Concerns, by Suzanne M. Kirchhoff.

[3] The Food and Drug Administration defines a brand-name drug as a drug marketed under a proprietary, trademark-protected name. See "Brand Name Drug," Drugs@FDA Glossary of Terms, at http://www.fda.gov/Drugs/InformationOnDrugs/ucm079436.htm#B.

[4] IMS Institute for Healthcare Informatics, Medicines Use and Spending Shifts: A Review of the Use of Medicines in the U.S. in 2014, April 2015, p. 25, at http://www.imshealth.com/portal/site/imshealth/menuitem.762a961826aad98f53c753c71ad8c22a/?vgnextoid=3f140a4331e8c410VgnVCM1000000e2e2ca2RCRD&vgnextchannel=736de5fda6370410VgnVCM10000076192ca2RCRD&vgnextfmt=default.

[5] Mason Tenaglia, "Copay Cards and Coupons: Letting Facts Get in the Way," Pharmaceutical Executive, January 1, 2012, at http://www.pharmexec.com/pharmexec/Commentary/Copay-Cards-and-Coupons-Letting-the-Facts-Get-in-t/ArticleStandard/Article/detail/755091. For example, North Carolina-based firm Trialcard manages more than $1 billion in patient reimbursement annually through co-payment programs for more than 140 brands and 60 manufacturers. See Trialcard, "Patient Affordability Services," at http://corp. trialcard.com/Pages/PatientAffordability.aspx.

[6] Health care payers include commercial insurers, unions and employers, and government programs.

[7] PhRMA, "Copay Coupons, Get the Full Story," June 22, 2012, at http://www.phrma.org/copay-coupons-get-the-fullstory/.

[8] Stacie Dusetzina, Aaron Winn, Gregory Abel, Haiden Huskamp, and Nancy Keating, "Cost Sharing and Adherence to Tyrosine Kinase Inhibitors for Patients With Chronic Myeloid Leukemia," Journal of Clinical Oncology, December 23, 2013, at http://jco.ascopubs.org/content/early/2013/12/23/JCO.2013.52.9123.

[9] David Grande, "The Cost of Drug Coupons," The Journal of the American Medical Association (vol. 307, no. 22), June 13, 2012, at http://jama.jamanetwork.com/article.aspx? Articleid =1182868; and Department of Health and Human Services (HHS), Office of Inspector General (OIG), Manufacturer Safeguards May Not Prevent Copayment Coupon Use for Part D Drugs, September 2014, at http://oig.hhs.gov/oei/reports/oei-05-12-00540.pdf. In addition, payers often negotiate additional rebates or other price concessions from drug companies based on the volume of specific drugs used by their enrollees. If enrollees switch to other drugs, based on coupon offers, the payers might not realize the expected financial benefits of the volume-based agreements.

[10] HHS, OIG, "Special Advisory Bulletin: Pharmaceutical Manufacturer Copayment Coupons," September 2014, at http://oig.hhs.gov/fraud/docs/alertsandbulletins/2014/SAB_Copayment_Coupons.pdf; Lara Maggs and Aaron Kesselheim, "The Short-Term and Long-Term Outlook Of Drug Coupons," Health Affairs Blog, November 12, 2014, at http://healthaffairs.org/blog/2014/11/12/the-short-term-and-long-term-outlook-of-drug-coupons/.

[11] See, generally, CRS Report RS22743, Health Care Fraud and Abuse Laws Affecting Medicare and Medicaid: An Overview, by Jennifer A. Staman.

[12] CRS Report R40611, Medicare Part D Prescription Drug Benefit, by Suzanne M. Kirchhoff and Patricia A. Davis.

[13] See text box entitled "Common Insurance Terms," below.

[14] Express Scripts, "Smart Formulary Management," January 2, 2014, at http://lab.express-scripts.com/insights/drugoptions/smart-formulary-management. The preferred formulary is selected by about 30% of health care payer clients Express Scripts serves. Suzanne Shelley, "Copay Programs' Increased Value to Manufacturers is Matched by Rising Criticism," Pharmaceutical Commerce, January 15, 2014, at http://www.pharmaceuticalcommerce.com/latest_news?articleid=27073&keyword=copay%20programs-insurance-coupons-pharmacy.

[15] Centers for Disease Control and Prevention, National Center for Health Statistics (NCHS), 2013 NCHS Chartbook: Special Feature on Prescription Drugs, at http://www.cdc.gov/nchs/hus/chartbook.htm#chartbook_special_feature; and Centers for Medicare & Medicaid Services (CMS), "Projections of National Health Expenditures: Methodology and Model Specifications," September 3, 2014, p. 27, at http://www.cms.gov/Research-Statistics-Data-and-Systems/Statistics-Trends-and-Reports/NationalHealthExpendData/Downloads/ProjectionsMethodology.pdf.

[16] CMS, "National Health Expenditure Data," at https://www.cms.gov/Research-Statistics-Data-and-Systems/StatisticsTrends-and-Reports/NationalHealthExpendData/NationalHealthAccountsHistorical.html.The National Health Expenditure drug estimates are based on U.S. Census Bureau and IMS Health drug data. The figures include retail sales of prescription drugs, subtract manufacturer rebates, and add government spending for drugs provided by government-owned mail-order facilities. They do not include drugs dispensed in institutional settings such as hospitals or clinics. See CMS, "National Health Expenditure Accounts Methodology Paper 2010: Definitions, Sources and Methods," at http://www.cms.gov/Research-Statistics-Data-and-Systems/Statistics-Trends-and-Reports/NationalHealthExpendData/downloads/dsm-10.pdf. For example, less than 2% of the U.S. population used prescription drugs to control high blood pressure from 1988 to 1994, compared with 12.5% from 2007 to 2010. For those aged 65 and older, the percentage rose from 5.9% to 46.7% during that period.

[17] See CMS, National Health Expenditure Accounts Methodology Paper, 2013, p. 15, at https://www.cms.gov/Research-Statistics-Data-and-Systems/Statistics-Trends-and-Reports/NationalHealthExpendData/downloads/dsm13.pdf. The CMS data define out-of-pocket spending as direct consumer spending for services not covered by insurance and the amount of coinsurance or deductibles required by private health insurance and public programs such as Medicare and Medicaid (not paid by some other third party), as well as payments covered by health savings accounts linked to high-deductible health plans. Premium payments are not included in out-of-pocket costs.

[18] CMS, "National Health Expenditure Data," at https://www.cms.gov/Research-Statistics-Data-and-Systems/StatisticsTrends-and-Reports/NationalHealthExpendData/NationalHealthAccountsHistorical.html.

[19] Among notable prescription drug legislation, Congress has enacted the voluntary Medicare Part D prescription drug program (Medicare Modernization Act of 2003, P.L. 108-173), and the 2010 Patient Protection and Affordable Care Act (ACA; P.L. 111-148), which also expanded Medicaid coverage. See CRS Report R41125, Medicaid and CHIP: Changes Made by the Health Care and Education Reconciliation Act of 2010 (HCERA, P.L. 111-152) to the Patient Protection and Affordable Care Act (PPACA, P.L. 111-148), coordinated by Evelyne P. Baumrucker and Cliff Binder.

[20] Thomas Oliver, Philip Lee, and Helene Lipton, "A Political History of Medicare and Prescription Drug Coverage," The Milbank Quarterly, (vol. 82. no. 2, June 2004, pp 283–354, http://www.ncbi.nlm.nih.gov/pmc/articles/PMC2690175/.

[21] Cynthia Smith, "Retail Spending in the National Health Accounts," Health Affairs, vol. 23, no. 1 (January/February 2004), pp. 160-167.

[22] CMS, "National Health Expenditure Data," at https://www.cms.gov/Research-Statistics-Data-and-Systems/StatisticsTrends-and-Reports/NationalHealthExpendData/NationalHealth AccountsHistorical.html. More than 99% of covered workers in employer-sponsored plans in 2014 were in a plan that had a prescription drug benefit. Kaiser Family Foundation, 2014 Employer Health Benefits Survey: Section Nine: Prescription Drug Benefits, September 10, 2014, at http://kff. org/health-costs/report/2014-employer-health-benefits-survey/.

[23] CMS, National Health Expenditure Projections, 2014-2024, Forecast Summary, at http://www.cms.gov/ResearchStatistics-Data-and-Systems/Statistics-Trends-and-Reports/NationalHealthExpendData/Downloads/proj2014.pdf. Even with the increase, out-of-pocket spending will decline as a share of overall prescription drug spending as Medicare spending grows.

[24] A high-deductible health plan (HDHP) has a higher deductible than traditional insurance products. For example, in 2015, Internal Revenue Service (IRS) regulations allow contributions to tax-advantaged savings accounts for enrollees in HDHPs, which are defined as plans with a minimum annual deductible of $1,300 for individual coverage and $2,600 for family coverage. The IRS also imposes limits on out-of-pocket spending under the plans. See IRS, Rev. Proc. 2014 30, at https://www.irs.gov/pub/irs-drop/rp-14-30.pdf.

[25] IMS Health, Medicine and the Shifting Costs of Healthcare, April 2014, p. 26.

[26] See Express Scripts, "U.S. Rx Spending Increased 13.1% in 2014," March 10, 2015, at http://lab.express-scripts.com/insights/industry-updates/us-rx-spending-increased-13-per cent-in-2014. Express Scripts said specialty drugs made up 31.8% of total U.S. drug spending in 2014.

[27] IMS Institute for Healthcare Informatics, Medicine Use and Shifting Costs of Healthcare: A Review of the Use of Medicines in the U.S. in 2013, April 2014, p. 40, at http://www. imshealth.com/portal/site/imshealth/menuitem.762a961826aad98f53c753c71ad8c22a/?vgne xtoid=2684d47626745410VgnVCM10000076192ca2RCRD. IMS Institute, Medicines Use and Spending Shifts: A Review of the Use of Medicines in the U.S. in 2014, April 2015, p. 8, at http://www.imshealth. com/portal/site/imshealth/menuitem.762a961826aad98f53c753c 71ad8c22a/?vgnextoid=3f140a4331e8c410VgnVCM1000000e2e2ca2RCRD&vgnextchann el=736de5fda6370410VgnVCM10000076192ca2RCRD&vgnextfmt=default.UnitedHealthc are Center for Health Reform & Modernization, The Growth of Specialty Pharmacy: Current Trends and Future Opportunities, April 2014, p. 1, at http://www.unitedhealth group.com/Modernization/KeyIssues/SpecialtyPharmacy.aspx. U.S. health care spending grew by a projected 5.5% in 2014, while prescription drug spending rose by 12.6%, driven by specialty drugs and increased prescription drug use. CMS, "National Health Expenditure Projections 2014-2024," p. 2, at http://www.cms.gov/Research-Statistics-Data-and-Systems/ Statistics-Trends-and-Reports/NationalHealthExpendData/Downloads/proj2014.pdf.

[28] According to a survey by America's Health Insurance Plans (AHIP), there were nearly 17.4 million enrollees in HDHPs with health savings accounts (HSAs) in January 2014, up from 11.4 million in January 2011. HDHPs have grown 15% annually on average since 2011. AHIP, "New Census Survey Shows Increased Growth in HSA Enrollment," July 9, 2014, at https://www.ahip.org/Press-Room/2014/HSA-Census-Survey/. HDHP enrollees may pay for drugs and other services with HSAs or may have access to other, employer-provided

health reimbursement. See CRS Report RS21573, Tax-Advantaged Accounts for Health Care Expenses: Side-by-Side Comparison, 2013, by Carol Rapaport.

[29] Peter J. Huckfeldt et al., "Patient Responses to Incentives in Consumer-Directed Health Plans: Evidence from Pharmaceuticals," National Bureau of Economic Research Working Paper 20927, February 2015, at http://www.nber.org/papers/w20927.pdf.

[30] Kaiser Family Foundation, "Medical and Prescription Drug Deductibles for Plans Offered in Federally Facilitated and Partnership Marketplaces for 2015," November 18, 2014, at http://kff.org/health-reform/fact-sheet/medical-andprescription-drug-deductibles-for-plans-offered-in-federally-facilitated-and-partnership-marketplaces-for-2015/. The study looked at insurance plans that imposed separate medical and drug deductibles.

[31] IMS Institute for Healthcare Informatics, Emergence and Impact of Pharmacy Deductibles: Implications for Patients in Commercial Health Plans, September 2015, p. 17.

[32] Insurers also use other prescription drug cost controls, often in conjunction with tiered pricing, including 1) requiring physicians and enrollees to obtain preauthorization for certain prescriptions; 2) imposing step therapy, where enrollees must first try a less expensive drug before moving to a higher-cost product; 3) creating preferred pharmacy networks where enrollees pay less for drugs if they agree to patronize a small number of designated drugstores; 4) requiring enrollees to use mail-order pharmacies; 5) creating tight formularies (lists of covered drugs); or 6) limiting the amount of drugs that may dispensed in an initial prescription. See CRS Report R44132, Specialty Drugs: Background and Policy Concerns, by Suzanne M. Kirchhoff.

[33] A generic drug is identical to a brand-name drug in dosage form, safety, strength, route of administration, quality, performance characteristics, and intended use. Although generic drugs are chemically identical to their branded counterparts, they are typically sold at substantial discounts from the branded price. According to the Congressional Budget Office, generic drugs save consumers an estimated $8 billion to $10 billion a year at retail pharmacies. Even more billions of dollars are saved when hospitals use generics. For more information, see CRS Report RL33605, Authorized Generic Pharmaceuticals: Effects on Innovation, by John R. Thomas.

[34] The tiering system can be fluid. For example, with prices for some generic drugs increasing, insurers are instituting preferred and non-preferred generic tiers or placing higher-cost generics on what had been a brand-name tier and moving some lower-priced brand-name drugs down to what had been a generic tier.

[35] Kaiser Family Foundation, 2014 Employer Health Benefits Survey: Section Nine: Prescription Drug Benefits, September 10, 2014, at http://kff.org/health-costs/report/2014-employer-health-benefits-survey/.

[36] CMS, "Medicare Part D Specialty Tier," April 7, 2014, at https://www.cms.gov/Medicare/Prescription-DrugCoverage/PrescriptionDrugCovGenIn/Downloads/SpecialtyTierMethodology.pdf.

[37] Shelly Carrey, Pharmacy Benefit Management Institute, "8 Ways Pharmacy Benefit Design May Evolve in 2013," Institute for Health Care Consumerism, at http://www.theihcc.com/en/communities/pharmacy_benefit_management/8-ways-pharmacy-benefit-design-may-evolve-in-2013_hfpq9mpi.html.

[38] Kaiser Family Foundation, 2014 Employer Health Benefits Survey, Section Nine, Exhibit 9.4, at http://kff.org/reportsection/ehbs-2014-section-nine-prescription-drug-benefits/. There were also wider differentials in coinsurance percentages between tiers for insurers requiring coinsurance.

[39] Charles River Associates, "The Economics of Co-Pay Coupons, CRA Insights: Life Sciences," November 2014, at http://www.crai.com/sites/default/files/publications/LS-Insights-Litigation-The-economics-of-copay-coupons1114_0.pdf.

[40] Avalere, "Exchange Plans Increase Costs of Specialty Drugs for Patients in 2015," December 2, 2014, at http://avalere.com/news/exchange-plans-increase-costs-of-specialty-drugs-for-patients-in-2015.

[41] Ibid and CMS, "Patient Protection and Affordable Care Act; HHS Notice of Benefit and Payment Parameters for 2016," 79 Federal Register 70673, November 21, 2014, at https://www.federalregister.gov/articles/2014/11/26/2014-27858/patient-protection-and-affordable-care-act-hhs-notice-of-benefit-and-payment-parameters-for-2016.

[42] Kaiser Family Foundation, 2014 Employer Health Benefits Survey: Section Seven: Employee Cost Sharing, September 10, 2014, at http://kff.org/health-costs/report/2014-employer-health-benefits-survey/.

[43] Generic drugs can cost 70%-80% less than their brand-name alternatives. See CRS Report RL33605, Authorized Generic Pharmaceuticals: Effects on Innovation, by John R. Thomas. Aggressive discounting may reduce a manufacturer's profit margin on a drug but result in a greater volume of sales. A 2012 study by the Amundsen Group, a health care consulting firm, estimated that co-payment offset programs produced manufacturer returns on investment of about 4 to1 and as much as 6 to 1. According to the firm, a well-designed coupon program could add 30 days to 60 days of patient drug use during a year. Mason Tenaglia, "Copay Cards and Coupons: Letting Facts Get in the Way," Pharmaceutical Executive, January 1, 2012, at http://www.pharmexec.com/pharmexec/Commentary/Copay-Cards-andCoupons-Letting-the-Facts-Get-in-t/ArticleStandard/Article/detail/755091.

[44] Insurers and pharmacy benefit managers negotiate rebates and discounts from manufacturers on the drugs that they purchase for health plans or distribute through their own mail-order and specialty pharmacies. These rebates and discounts are separate from those that manufacturers offer consumers through coupons and other assistance programs. Overall drug pricing also includes payments to pharmacies that dispense the drugs and other costs and markups along the supply chain, but those costs have been kept out to simplify the transaction.

[45] Trialcard, "Leveraging Data and Analytics to Enhance Copay Program Performance," Pharmaceutical Executive, special advertising section.

[46] HHS, OIG, "Manufacturer Safeguards May Not Prevent Copayment Coupon Use for Part D Drugs," September 2014, p. 5, at http://oig.hhs.gov/oei/reports/oei-05-12-00540.pdf.

[47] Lash Group, Amerisource Bergen, "Co-Pay Mechanisms: Which Card is Right for Your Product?" Available with registration at http://www.lashgroup.com/resource-center/copay-assistance.

[48] National Council for Prescription Drug Programs, "Transformation and the Use of HIT in Pharmacy," https://www.ncpdp.org/NCPDP/media/pdf/wp/RxforImprovingHealthcare_Transformation HIT.pdf.

[49] HHS, OIG, Manufacturer Safeguards May Not Prevent Copayment Coupon Use for Part D Drugs, September 2014, at http://oig.hhs.gov/oei/reports/oei-05-12-00540.pdf.

[50] Ibid.

[51] MedImpact/ScriptSave power point, October 28, 2014, at http://medimpactpbm.com/v/kbuua8wbmynec3rsl6pe. Some health care consultants have designed integrated programs in which insurance plan enrollees can use a preprogrammed card to pay for drugs covered

by their insurance benefit and to access coupon offers for products that are not included on a plan formulary.

[52] Zitter Health Insights, "Co-Pay Offset Monitor Environmental Report," PhRMA, March 2015. Made available to CRS by Zitter Health Insights.

[53] IMS Health, "Patient Savings Program Use Analysis," February 2014, at http://www.imshealth.com/portal/site/imshealth/menuitem.0be132395225d98ee566e5661ad8c22a/?vgnextoid=a64de5fda637041OVgnVCM10000076192ca2RCRD&vgnextfmt=default. The study was funded by drug manufacturer Pfizer. It is based on IMS Health anonymized patient longitudinal prescription data as reported by retail pharmacies and did not include mail-order or other non-retail pharmacies. The patient savings programs were limited to those with 100 or more unique patients assisted during the 12-month period ending October 31, 2012.

[54] Mason Tenaglia, "Copay Cards and Coupons: Letting Facts Get in the Way," Pharmaceutical Executive, January 1, 2012, at http://www.pharmexec.com/pharmexec/Commentary/Copay-Cards-and-Coupons-Letting-the-Facts-Get-in-t/ArticleStandard/Article/detail/755091.

[55] IMS Institute for Healthcare Informatics, "Patient Savings Program Use Analysis," February 2014; Chris Dowd, "Broadening Your Co-Pay Approach," PM 360, April 30, 2015, at http://www.pm360online.com/broadening-your-copay-approach/.

[56] Jonathan Rockoff, "Goodbye, Lipitor. Pfizer Bids a Farewell," Wall Street Journal, May 9, 2012, at http://www.wsj.com/articles/SB10001424052702304543904577394263634380548.

[57] Trialcard, "How the Affordable Care Act Made Co-pay Programs a Requirement for Patient Access," 2014. Available for download with registration at http://corp.trialcard.com/Pages/WhitePaper.aspx; and Lash Group, AmeriSource Bergen, "How Simplified Co-Pay Processes Increased Regimen Adherence by 30%." Available for download with registration at http://www.lashgroup.com/resource-center/copay-assistance.

[58] IMS Health/Amundsen, "Co-Pay Offset Program Case Study," April 2014, at http://www.amundsengroup.com/capabilitiescase-studiesco-pay-offset-program-case-study/. Manufacturers may ask consumers to provide certain information as a condition for receiving a coupon.

[59] Andrew Pollack, "Cancer Doctors Offer Way to Compare Medicines, Including by Cost," New York Times, June 22, 2015, at http://www.nytimes.com/2015/06/23/business/cancer-doctors-offer-way-to-compare-medicines-including-bycost.html.

[60] Physicians Interactive, "eCouponing," 2015. Available with registration at http://www.physiciansinteractive.com/resources/ecouponing-delivering-greater-value-in-the-clinicians-prescribing-workflow/. OptimizeRx, "About OptimizeRx Corporation," at http://www.optimizerx.com/about/index.php and "OptimizeRx Corp. and Allscripts Expand Partnership to Automate Savings Within EHR to Improve Patient Adherence," Marketwired, August 3, 2015, at http://www.marketwired.com/press-release/optimizerx-corp-allscripts-expand-partnership-automate-savings-withinehr-improve-patient-otcqb-oprx-2044400.htm.

[61] Physicians Interactive, "Physicians Interactive and McKesson Announce Partnership to Provide Coupons on DemandTM," March 4, 2014, at http://www.physician sinteractive.com/news/physicians-interactive-and-mckessonannounce-partnership-to-provide-coupons-on-demand/.

[62] Consumer Reports, "A Drugstore Tool We're Not Crazy About," December 2012, at http://www.consumerreports.org/cro/2012/12/a-drugstore-tool-we-re-not-crazy-about/index.htm.

[63] Good Rx, http://www.goodrx.com/.

[64] §1128B(b) of the Social Security Act.

[65] The HHS OIG in October 2014 issued proposed regulations that would create safe harbors from the antikickback statute for certain Part D program activities. For example, the proposed rules would provide protection for pharmacy waivers of cost sharing for financially needy Medicare Part D beneficiaries and for mandatory manufacturer discounts in the Part D coverage gap. HHS, OIG, 42 C.F.R. Parts 1001 and 1003, "Medicare and State Health Care Programs: Fraud and Abuse; Revisions to Safe Harbors Under the Anti-Kickback Statute, and Civil Monetary Penalty Rules Regarding Beneficiary Inducements and Gainsharing," 79 Federal Register 59717, October 3, 2014, at https://www.federalregister.gov/articles/2014/10/03/2014-23182/medicare-and-state-health-care-programs-fraud-andabuse-revisions-to-safe-harbors-under-the#h-4.

[66] 31 U.S.C. §§3729-3733. See also 42 U.S.C. §1320a-7b(g).

[67] U.S. Department of Justice, "KMART Corporation Pays $1.4 Million to Resolve False Claims Act Allegations in Connection with Drug Manufacturer Coupons and Gas Discounts," September 1, 2015, at http://www.justice.gov/opa/pr/kmart-corporation-pays-14-million-resolve-false-claims-act-allegations-connection-drug.

[68] See 42 U.S.C. §1320a-7b(f)(1). See also Office of Personnel Management, "Frequently Asked Questions: Insurance," at http://www.opm.gov/faqs/QA.aspx?fid=fd635746-de0a-4dd7-997d-b5706a0fd8d2&pid=c8263db8-cf0e4144-9e8a-13a1ef38c084.

[69] An ACA-qualified health plan is an insurance plan that is certified by a state exchange, provides essential health benefits, follows established limits on cost sharing (such as deductibles, co-payments, and out-of-pocket maximum amounts), and meets other requirements. See https://www.healthcare.gov/glossary/qualified-health-plan/.

[70] Letter from Kathleen Sebelius, HHS Secretary, to Rep. McDermott, October 2014, at http://gallery.mailchimp.com/31e15e5fee7b5a6208b646806/files/The_Honorable_Jim_McDermott.pdf?utm_source=Arent+Fox+List&utm_campaign=19e4815037-20131104_Legal_Alert_DHHS&utm_medium=email&utm_term=0_3a013c8d3d19e4815037-.

[71] Letter from Kathleen Sebelius to Sen. Charles Grassley, February 12, 2014, at http://online.wsj.com/public/resources/documents/GrassleyLetter0219.pdf.

[72] CRS Legal Sidebar WSLG246, Earning Rewards when Buying Drugs Covered by Medicare and Medicaid: HHS Gives the Green Light, by Jennifer A. Staman.

[73] HHS, OIG, "Medicare and State Health Care Programs: Fraud and Abuse; Revisions to Safe Harbors Under the Anti-Kickback Statute, and Civil Monetary Penalty Rules Regarding Beneficiary Inducements and Gainsharing," 79 Federal Register 59717, October 3, 2014, at https://www.federalregister.gov/articles/2014/10/03/2014-23182/medicare-andstate-health-care-programs-fraud-and-abuse-revisions-to-safe-harbors-under-the#h-4.

[74] In July 2014, the HHS OIG issued an advisory opinion regarding a direct-to-patient sales program sponsored by a specific pharmaceutical manufacturer under which an individual may buy a prescription drug at a fixed cash price through an online pharmacy. The offer is open to patients who have a valid prescription and are uninsured, have commercial prescription drug insurance, or are enrolled in Medicare Part D or other federal programs. The product is sold outside of all federal drug benefits. The manufacturer does not enter into rebate agreements with third-party payers and requires patients to provide full information regarding insurance status. HHS ruled that in this limited case, even though the arrangement could potentially generate prohibited remuneration under the antikickback statute, it would not impose administrative sanctions against the company. HHS, OIG, "OIG Advisory Opinion 14-05," July 28, 2014, at https://oig.hhs.gov/compliance/advisory-opinions/. CMS

has also issued separate guidance for Part D cash purchases at out-of-network pharmacies where coupon use is not involved. See CMS, "Understanding True Out-of-Pocket (TrOOP) Costs," at https://www.cms.gov/Outreach-and-Education/Outreach/Partnerships/downloads/11223-P.pdf; and CMS, Medicare Part D Prescription Drug Manual, Chapter 14, Section 50.4.2, at https://www.cms.gov/Medicare/Prescription-Drug-Coverage/PrescriptionDrugCovContra/Downloads/Chapter14.pdf.

[75] Tracy Staton, "Pfizer launches next new Lipitor copay program, Medicare and ACA included," FiercePharma, June 2, 2014, at www.fiercepharmamarketing.com/story/pfizer-launches-next-new-lipitor-copay-program-medicard-andaca-included/2014-06-02. Also see "About the Lipitor Choice Card" at https://www.lipitor.com/choice-card.

[76] HHS, OIG, Manufacturer Safeguards May Not Prevent Copayment Coupon Use for Part D Drugs, September 2014, at http://oig.hhs.gov/oei/reports/oei-05-12-00540.pdf.

[77] For example, an individual could be enrolled in Part D but not yet have met the annual deductible. The individual's coverage would not begin until he or she meets the deductible.

[78] HHS, OIG, "Special Advisory Bulletin: Pharmaceutical Manufacturer Copayment Coupons," September 2014, at http://oig.hhs.gov/fraud/docs/alertsandbulletins/2014/SAB_Copayment_Coupons.pdf.

[79] Pharmacy Benefits Management Institute, Prescription Drug Benefit Cost and Plan Design Report 2014-2015 Edition, p. 27. Report is sponsored by Takeda Pharmaceuticals. Data are based on a survey of 353 employers representing more than 29 million members. Larger employers are those that cover more than 5,000 lives, and smaller employers are those that cover fewer than 5,000 lives. The survey was conducted in April 2014.

[80] The Pink Sheet Daily, "UnitedHealthcare Program Will Bar Copay Coupons For Six Specialty Drugs," October 26, 2012. In March 2014, UnitedHealthcare said it would partner with retail pharmacies to discontinue the use of co-payment coupons. However, in April 2014 the insurer said it would delay the initiative. UnitedHealthcare, "July 1, 2014, Retail Coupons Policy," at http://broker.uhc.com/assets/Coupon%20Policy.pdf; and UnitedHealthcare, "Pharmacy Retail Coupon Update," April 11, 2014, at http://broker.uhc.com/articleView-13383.

[81] Express Scripts, "Smart Formulary Management," January 2, 2014, at http://lab.express-scripts.com/insights/drugoptions/smart-formulary-management. The preferred formulary is selected by about 30% of Express Scripts clients.

[82] IMS Health, "Maintaining Patient Access to Affordable Medication through OPUS Health's DebitRxTM Solution," at http://www.rm.imshealth.com/Docs_CaseStudies/Marketing/DebitRx_CaseStudy_Rheumatoid-Arthritis.pdf. Opus Health is owned by IMS.

[83] Community Catalyst, "Current Lawsuits," at http://www.communitycatalyst.org/initiatives-and-issues/initiatives/prescription-access-litigation/current-lawsuits; David McAfee, "Merck Escapes Suits Over Prescription Copay Coupons," law360, April 29, 2013, at http://www.law360.com/articles/437025/merck-escapes-suits-over-prescriptioncopay-coupons; and Paul Milford and Dawn McCarty, "Pfizer, Abbott, Glaxo Sued Over Brand-Drug Co-Pay Discounts," Bloomberg, March 7, 2012, at http://www.bloomberg.com/news/2012-03-07/pfizer-abbott-faceallegations-over-co-pay-coupon-promotions.html.

[83] New England Carpenters Health and Welfare Fund vs. Abbott Laboratories and Abbie, U.S. District Court for the Northern District of Illinois, Eastern Division, Case No. 12 CV 1662, at http://www.policymed.com/2014/10/federalcourt-dismisses-rico-allegations-pharmaceutical- manufacturers-and-pharmacies-not-in-racketee.html.

[84] Catherine Starner, G. Caleb Alexander, Kevin Bowen, Yang Qiu, Peter Wickersham, and Patrick Gleason, "Specialty Drug Coupons Lower Out-Of-Pocket Costs And May Improve

Adherence At The Risk Of Increasing Premiums," Health Affairs, vol. 33, no. 10 (October 2014), pp. 1761-1769.

[85] Mason Tenaglia, "Copay Cards and Coupons: Letting Facts Get in the Way," Pharmaceutical Executive, January 1, 2012, at http://www.pharmexec.com/pharmexec/Commentary/Copay-Cards-and-Coupons-Letting-the-Facts-Get-in-t/ArticleStandard/Article/detail/755091.

[86] Jonas Daugherty, Matthew Maciejewski, and Joel Farley, "The Impact of Manufacturer Coupon Use in the Statin Market," Journal of Managed Care Pharmacy, vol. 19, no. 9 (October 2013). The study used commercially available claims data spanning three years and representing 340,350 patients to compare demographics, statin use, and expenditures of patients initiating generic statins, brand-name statins without manufacturer coupons, and brand-name statins with manufacturer coupons. The number of statin fills in the 12 months following initiation was highest for coupon users, slightly lower for patients initiating generic statins, and lowest for non-coupon users. Coupon users had higher total statin prescription costs than generic initiators and non-coupon users ($798 vs. $92 vs. $678) and higher pre-coupon out-of-pocket costs ($339 vs. $53 vs. $169; P<0.001). Health plan costs for statins excluding rebates were lower for coupon users than non-coupon users ($460 vs. $508; P<0.001) but much higher compared with generic statin initiators ($460 vs. $39).

[87] Catherine Starner et al., "Specialty Drug Coupons Lower Out-Of-Pocket Costs And May Improve Adherence At The Risk Of Increasing Premiums," Health Affairs, vol. 33, no. 10 (October 2014), pp. 1761-1769. The study examined 264,801 specialty drug prescriptions in 2013 covered by the insurance plans it served. Spending for the specialty claims totaled $911.8 million, of which $35.3 million (3.9%) was paid out of pocket by enrollees. Beneficiaries used coupons for 44.3% of the prescriptions, which offset $21.2 million (60.2%) of the $35.3 million in charges. In most cases, the coupons reduced monthly out-of-pocket costs to less than $250, a price at which Prime Therapeutics said separate data indicated that patients using high-cost drugs were less likely to abandon therapy.

[88] According to the FDA, drug products classified as therapeutically equivalent can be substituted with the full expectation that the substituted product will produce the same clinical effect and safety profile as the prescribed product. Drugs must meet specific guidelines to be deemed therapeutically equivalent. See http://www.fda.gov/Drugs/InformationOnDrugs/ucm079436.htm#T.

[89] Joseph Ross and Aaron Kesselheim, "Prescription-Drug Coupons—No Such Thing as a Free Lunch," New England Journal of Medicine, vol. 369, no. 13 (September 26, 2013), at http://www.nejm.org/doi/full/10.1056/NEJMp1301993.

[90] For illustrative descriptions see CMS, "Pharmaceutical Manufacturer Patient Assistance Program," at http://www.cms.gov/Medicare/Prescription-Drug-Coverage/PrescriptionDrugCovGenIn/PAPData.html and National Alliance of Mental Illness, at http://www.nami.org/Content/ContentGroups/Helpline1/Prescription_Drug_Patient_Assistance_Programs.htm.

[91] Suzanne Shelley, "Pharma Struggles to Manage the Complexity of its Patient Assistance Programs," Pharmaceutical Commerce, February 26, 2013, at http://pharmaceuticalcommerce.com/brand_communications?articleid=26770.

[92] To qualify, individuals often must have annual incomes below 200% of the federal poverty level.

[93] See Partnership for Prescription Assistance at https://www.pparx.org/about_us/patient_advocates.

[94] CMS, "Prescription Drug Assistance Programs," at http://www.cms.gov/Medicare/Coordination -of-Benefits-andRecovery/Prescription-Drug-Assistance-Programs/Overview.html.

[95] Medicare.gov, "Pharmaceutical Assistance Programs," at http://www.medicare.gov/pharmaceutical-assistanceprogram/. See also https://www.pparx.org/prescription_assistance_programs/list_of_participating_programs.

[96] See RxAssist at http://www.rxassist.org/faqs.

[97] CMS, "Pharmaceutical Manufacturer Patient Assistance Program Information," at http://www.cms.gov/Medicare/Prescription-Drug-Coverage/PrescriptionDrugCovGenIn/PAPData.html.

[98] In December 2014, the HHS OIG issued another advisory opinion regarding a specific PAP targeted at people suffering from Crohn's Disease and ulcerative colitis. Under the proposed program, a nonprofit group would provide co-payment and other assistance to financially needy patients on a first-come, first-served basis. Before receiving the aid, patients would choose their own doctor and their specific medication. The program would be funded from a variety of sources, including drug manufacturers, but the funders would not have influence over the program, according to information submitted to HHS. The OIG determined that because of the way the PAP was structured—with no donor exerting direct control, patients choosing their own course of treatment, and limited exchange of patient information— it posed a very low risk for potential fraud and abuse. HHS OIG, "Re: OIG Advisory Opinion No. 14-11," December 29, 2014, at https://oig.hhs.gov/fraud/docs/advisoryopinions/2014/AdvOpn14-11.pdf.

[99] HHS, OIG, "Supplemental Special Advisory Bulletin: Independent Charity Patient Assistance Programs," 79 Federal Register 31120-31123, at http://oig.hhs.gov/fraud/docs/alertsandbulletins/2014/independent-charity-bulletin.pdf.

[100] Medicare.gov, "State Pharmaceutical Association Programs," at http://www.medicare.gov/pharmaceuticalassistance-program/state-programs. aspx.

[101] CRS Report R40611, Medicare Part D Prescription Drug Benefit, by Suzanne M. Kirchhoff and Patricia A. Davis.

[102] CRS Report R40425, Medicare Primer, coordinated by Patricia A. Davis and Scott R. Talaga.

[103] CRS Report R43778, Medicaid Prescription Drug Pricing and Policy, by Cliff Binder.

[104] CRS Report R43627, State Children's Health Insurance Program: An Overview, by Evelyne P. Baumrucker and Alison Mitchell.

[105] CRS Report R42747, Health Care for Veterans: Answers to Frequently Asked Questions, by Sidath Viranga Panangala.

[106] CMS, "Final HHS Notice of Benefit and Payment Parameters for 2016," February 20, 2015, at https://www.cms.gov/Newsroom/MediaReleaseDatabase/Fact-sheets/2015-Fact-sheets-items/2015-02-20.html.

In: Pharmaceutical Industry Developments
Editor: Kristy Bishop
ISBN: 978-1-63484-649-3

Chapter 3

MANUFACTURER SAFEGUARDS MAY NOT PREVENT COPAYMENT COUPON USE FOR PART D DRUGS*

Office of Inspector General

EXECUTIVE SUMMARY

Why We Did This Study

Pharmaceutical manufacturers offer copayment coupons to reduce or eliminate the cost of patients' out-of-pocket copayments for specific brand-name drugs. The anti-kickback statute prohibits the knowing and willful offer or payment of remuneration to a person to induce the purchase of any item or service for which payment may be made by a Federal health care program. Manufacturers may be liable under the anti-kickback statute if they offer coupons to induce the purchase of drugs paid for by Federal health care programs, including Medicare Part D. The anti-kickback statute applies to all Federal health care programs, but this study focused on Part D. The use of coupons by Medicare beneficiaries could impose significant costs on the Part D program because many coupons encourage beneficiaries to choose more expensive brand-name drugs over less expensive alternative drugs. In two

* This is an edited, reformatted and augmented version of a report, OEI-05-12-00540, issued by the U.S. Department of Health and Human Services, September 2014.

surveys by outside groups, approximately 6 percent to 7 percent of seniors surveyed reported using coupons to purchase prescription drugs.

How We Did This Study

To identify the safeguards pharmaceutical manufacturers employ to prevent their copayment coupons from being used for drugs paid for by Part D and to identify vulnerabilities in those safeguards, we surveyed 30 manufacturers of the top 100 Part D brand-name drugs with coupons and with the highest Medicare expenditures. We also reviewed selected safeguards offered for a purposive sample of those drugs. In addition, we interviewed staff at various organizations involved in pharmacy claims transactions to understand other vulnerabilities associated with coupon use in Part D.

What We Found

Pharmaceutical manufacturers' current safeguards may not prevent all copayment coupons from being used for drugs paid for by Part D. All surveyed manufacturers provide notices directed to beneficiaries and pharmacists that coupons may not be used in Federal health care programs. Most surveyed manufacturers use pharmacy claims edits to prevent coupons from being processed for drugs covered by Part D. Most of these edits may not prevent all coupons from being processed for Part D-covered drugs. Finally, Part D plans and other entities cannot identify coupons within pharmacy claims.

What We Recommend

The Office of Inspector General's concurrent Special Advisory Bulletin affirms that pharmaceutical manufacturers are at risk of sanctions if they fail to take appropriate steps to ensure that their copayment coupons do not induce the purchase of Federal health care programs items or services, including but not limited to, drugs paid for by Medicare Part D. For this reason, manufacturers may engage industry stakeholders and the Centers for Medicare & Medicaid Services (CMS) in an effort to identify a solution to ensure that coupons are not used for drugs paid for by Part D. CMS should cooperate with industry stakeholder efforts to improve the reliability of pharmacy claims edits and make coupons transparent. CMS concurred with our recommendation.

OBJECTIVES

1) To describe safeguards pharmaceutical manufacturers employ to prevent copayment coupon use for drugs paid for by Medicare Part D.
2) To identify vulnerabilities in these safeguards.
3) To identify any other vulnerabilities associated with copayment coupon use for drugs paid for by Medicare Part D.

BACKGROUND

Pharmaceutical manufacturers offer copayment coupons to reduce or eliminate the cost of patients' out-of-pocket copayments for specific brand-name drugs and thereby induce the purchase of those drugs. Although coupons reduce individual patients' immediate costs, coupons may increase the cost of prescription drugs for health insurers, including those offering Medicare prescription drug coverage through Part D plans.[1]

The anti-kickback statute prohibits knowing and willful solicitation, receipt, offer, or payment of remuneration to induce the purchase of any item or service for which payment may be made in whole or in part under a Federal health care program.[2] Pharmaceutical manufacturers may be liable under the anti-kickback statute if they offer coupons to induce the purchase of drugs paid for by Medicare Part D or any other Federal health care program.[3]

Recent surveys by outside organizations found that approximately 6 percent to 7 percent of surveyed seniors reported using manufacturer coupons toward their copayment for prescription drugs purchased through their Medicare prescription plans.[4,5] Applying these results to the population of 36 million Part D beneficiaries, the utilization of copayment coupons to obtain prescription drugs paid for by Part D could exceed 2 million beneficiaries.

Pharmaceutical manufacturers' use of coupons to reduce the cost-sharing obligations for Medicare Part D drugs could impose significant costs on Federal health care programs and taxpayers. A 2013 study from *The New England Journal of Medicine* found that 58 percent of coupons were for brand-name drugs for which a lower cost generic alternative was available.[6] If manufacturer coupons encourage Medicare beneficiaries to obtain more expensive brand-name drugs when lower cost alternatives are available, the coupon may reduce individual beneficiaries' immediate out-of-pocket costs but Part D plans' and the Part D program's costs may increase, ultimately increasing costs to taxpayers.[7]

Medicare Part D Cost Controls

CMS contracts with private insurance companies, called sponsors, to provide Part D prescription drug benefits for approximately 36 million beneficiaries.[8, 9] Sponsors use a variety of methods to control prescription drug coverage costs through the Part D program.

Part D Formularies

Sponsors can establish formularies, or lists of covered drugs, to give preference to more effective drugs over less effective drugs or less expensive drugs over more expensive drugs that treat the same condition. To drive utilization toward equally effective but less expensive drugs, formularies are generally organized into tiers, which have different beneficiary copayments for a prescription drug. Drugs in lower tiers are typically the least expensive and have the lowest beneficiary copayments. Drugs in the subsequent and ascending tiers are, in general, relatively more expensive and have increasing beneficiary copayments. For example, a lower tier drug is typically a low-cost generic drug for which a beneficiary might have a $5 or $10 copayment, while a higher tier drug is likely to be a more expensive brand-name drug for which a beneficiary might have a $45 copayment.

Generic Substitution

Sponsors can control prescription drug costs by requiring less expensive, chemically equivalent generic drugs to be substituted for costlier brand-name drugs. Generic substitution may reduce the amounts that both Part D plans and beneficiaries pay for covered drugs. For instance, the average brand-name drug prescription costs $89, while the average generic drug prescription costs $23, a difference of $66.[10]

Beneficiary Copayments in Part D

Beneficiaries, Part D plans, and CMS share Part D prescription drug coverage costs. Beneficiary cost sharing begins in the initial benefit stage, which beneficiaries reach after paying their deductible. Beneficiaries' cost-sharing responsibilities for covered drugs then change as they move through different stages of the Part D benefit.[11]

During the initial benefit stage, beneficiaries pay copayments for prescription drugs on the basis of factors such as whether the drug is a generic or a brand, which formulary tier the drug is on, and whether the pharmacy is preferred or nonpreferred by the Part D plan.[12, 13, 14]

After reaching an initial coverage limit set in statute, beneficiaries typically enter the coverage gap stage where their cost-sharing increases.15,[16] In this stage, in 2013, pharmaceutical manufacturers provided beneficiaries a 50-percent discount on applicable drugs (generally, covered brand-name drugs) at the point of sale.[17] For most generic drugs, in 2013, beneficiaries were responsible for 79 percent of the cost as their copayment.[18]

The coverage gap continues until beneficiaries' true out-of-pocket (TrOOP) spending reaches the annual TrOOP threshold.[19] Generally, for brand-name drugs, the full amount of drug costs, including the out-of-pocket amount beneficiaries paid, counts toward their TrOOP.[20] For generic drugs, only the out-of-pocket amount counts toward beneficiaries' TrOOP thresholds.

After reaching the TrOOP threshold, beneficiaries enter the catastrophic benefit stage.[21] During catastrophic coverage, the Part D program pays the majority of beneficiaries' drug costs and beneficiaries are generally responsible for limited cost sharing through copayments.

Copayment Coupons

Pharmaceutical manufacturers typically offer copayment coupons to insured patients to reduce or eliminate patients' out-of-pocket costs for specific brand-name drugs. Manufacturers may contract with coupon vendors to create and administer coupon programs on their behalf. ("Manufacturers" includes all manufacturers or vendors acting on their behalf.) A manufacturer may offer a coupon for a brand-name drug that reduces the copayment for that drug and makes it cheaper than the copayment for a competitor drug. For example, a coupon may reduce a patient's copayment for Brand Drug A from \$20 to \$4, making the copayment for the brand drug cheaper than the copayment for a generic equivalent, which may be $10. In some cases, the coupon eliminates the copayment altogether.

Pharmaceutical manufacturers may offer copayment coupons for several reasons. It has been reported that manufacturers may use coupons to try to retain market share when generic and other brand-name drugs that treat the same condition become available to patients. It also has been reported that manufacturers may use coupons to attract new patients who may be using an alternative therapy. Additionally, manufacturers indicate that they offer coupons to encourage patients to adhere to their prescription drug regimen. Finally, it has been reported that manufacturers may offer coupons to offset the high cost of specialty and biologic drugs, which may not have generic alternatives.[22]

Copayment coupons have become increasingly prevalent. In recent years, the number of coupons has increased from 86 in July 2009[23] to 525 in December 2012.[24] This increase may be related to competition from generic drugs. From 2009 to 2012, numerous "blockbuster" drugs—drugs that have generated $1 billion in sales—lost their patent protection. For many of those drugs, generic versions became available. The number of generic drugs the Food and Drug Administration (FDA) approved increased 27 percent between 2009 and 2012.[25]

Copayment Coupon Formats

Copayment coupons typically are available in four formats: (1) print coupons, (2) electronic coupons, (3) debit cards, and (4) direct reimbursements. Print coupons are printed cards or documents that the patient physically takes or sends to the pharmacy to purchase a prescription drug. Electronic coupons are cardless programs that evaluate prescription drug claims as they are submitted through the pharmacy claims transaction system, which applies copayment reductions. Debit cards include any prepaid and/or bank-authorized card that is processed at the point of sale to pay for some predetermined portion of the copayment. Direct reimbursements are any payments by a manufacturer offered directly to a patient for all or part of the patient's out-of-pocket cost for a purchased prescription drug. Direct reimbursements occur after a prescription drug is purchased and generally do not involve pharmacies.

Most coupons offered by manufacturers are typically in the format of print coupons. Manufacturers offer electronic coupons to a lesser extent. A small number of coupons are offered in the format of debit cards and direct reimbursements. See Table 1, on the next page, for a breakdown of the prevalence of coupon formats among 30 manufacturers surveyed by the Office of Inspector General (OIG).

Table 1. Coupon Formats for Manufacturers Surveyed by OIG

Coupon Format	Number of Manufacturers Offering	Percentage of All Coupons Offered by Manufacturers
Print	27	71%
Electronic	22	26%
Debit Card	9	2%
Direct Reimbursement	16	1%

Source: OIG analysis of pharmaceutical manufacturer survey responses, 2013.

Accessing Copayment Coupons

Patients commonly access copayment coupons in four ways. Patients may access or receive coupons from their prescribing physicians. Patients also may access coupons through Web sites and toll-free telephone numbers managed by manufacturers or companies hired to manage their coupon programs. Finally, patients may be given coupons by pharmacists filling their prescriptions.

Redeeming Copayment Coupons

Patients typically redeem copayment coupons at pharmacies when they purchase prescription drugs. However, patients do not always redeem coupons at pharmacies and may request reimbursements directly from the manufacturer after purchasing prescription drugs.

Copayment Coupons and Pharmacy Claims Processing

Copayment coupon claims are typically processed in the same way as payments received from a secondary insurance source using the National Council for Prescription Drug Programs (NCPDP) Telecommunication Standard D.0 for pharmacy claims. Using this standard format, all pharmacy claims, including coupon claims, are electronically routed from the pharmacy to various payers by companies known as “switches.” Once a claim is routed to a payer, the payer sends coverage and payment information back to the pharmacy through the switch.

The processing of primary insurance and coupon claims occurs in real time and involves several steps to coordinate payment for a single claim. First, a patient's primary insurance claim is processed, and the patient's copayment amount is determined. Second, the coupon claim is processed, and how much of the copayment the manufacturer will pay is determined. Finally, the patient pays the remaining copayment balance, if any. See Figure 1, on the next page, for an illustration of how primary insurance and coupon claims are processed.

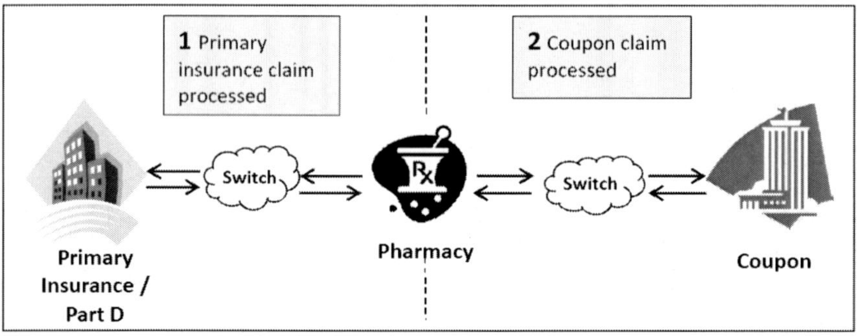

Source: OIG analysis of interview responses, 2013.

Figure 1. Processing of Primary Insurance and Coupon Claims.

The coordination of primary insurance and coupon or secondary payers is facilitated by unique identifiers that route the claim to the entity responsible for paying the claim. One identifier is the Bank Identification Number (BIN), which identifies the responsible payer. Primary insurers, including Part D plans, have BINs that route primary insurance claims to them for payment. Manufacturers also have BINs that route their coupon claims to them for payment. The Processor Control Number (PCN) is a secondary identifier that is internal to an insurance company or manufacturer and further routes the claim within that company.

To attempt to determine a patient's Part D enrollment status before submitting a coupon claim, a pharmacist may submit an optional enrollment verification request, called an E1 transaction, to the Part D Transaction Facilitator. CMS contracts with the Transaction Facilitator to track Part D beneficiaries' benefit stages and to conduct E1 transactions, which provide pharmacists with information about a patient's Part D enrollment status.[26] The pharmacist submits the patient's identification information to the Transaction Facilitator, which compares it to patient information in CMS's Medicare enrollment database to determine whether the patient is enrolled in Part D.

Pharmacies pay less than 1 cent per transaction to submit this verification request.[27]

METHODOLOGY

Scope

The anti-kickback statute applies to all Federal health care programs, but this study focused on Medicare Part D. This study analyzed the copayment coupon safeguards of pharmaceutical manufacturers for the most costly brand-name Part D prescription drugs with coupons covered in 2012. These prescription drugs were covered under stand-alone prescription drug plans and Medicare Advantage prescription drug plans. The study did not include coupons for generic drugs because copayment coupons are not commonly offered for generic drugs. This study did not estimate the use of coupons by Part D beneficiaries. It also did not estimate the overall cost of coupons to Part D plans and the Part D program.

Data Collection and Analysis

We collected information on safeguards pharmaceutical manufacturers employ to prevent copayment coupon use for drugs paid for by Medicare Part D through a survey of manufacturers and a review of copayment coupons and coupon Web sites. We collected information on other vulnerabilities through interviews with a variety of industry stakeholders.

We sent an online survey to 34 pharmaceutical manufacturers of drugs with coupons, and 30 responded. We selected these manufacturers by identifying the manufacturers offering the top 100 Part D-covered brand-name drugs with coupons by cost to Part D. The 30 complete surveys we received represented an 88-percent response rate. We analyzed survey responses to determine the extent to which manufacturers surveyed had safeguards in place to prevent the use of coupons for drugs paid for by Part D.

We also reviewed safeguards in place for a subset of the top 100 Part D-covered brand-name drugs with coupons. We attempted to obtain 50 coupons to determine the extent to which manufacturers had safeguards directed to beneficiaries and pharmacists in place. We reviewed these safeguards for the 40 coupons that we obtained.

In addition, we conducted structured interviews with staff at organizations involved in the pharmacy claims transaction process, including pharmacists, coupon vendors, a switching company, and NCPDP, to understand other vulnerabilities associated with coupon use in Part D.

For a discussion of our data collection and analysis, see Appendix A.

Data Limitations

Although we did not verify manufacturers' survey responses, we selected a sample of coupons offered by surveyed manufacturers to review safeguards on or associated with coupons. We used this information to confirm the accuracy of manufacturers' responses. We could not review safeguards that were not on coupons or on coupon Web sites. For these safeguards, this report relies on self-reported data.

Standards

This study was conducted in accordance with the *Quality Standards for Inspection and Evaluation* issued by the Council of the Inspectors General on Integrity and Efficiency.

FINDINGS

All Surveyed Manufacturers Provide Notices to Beneficiaries and Pharmacists That Copayment Coupons May Not Be Used in Federal Health Care Programs

All manufacturers surveyed report providing notices directed to Federal health care program beneficiaries or pharmacists for at least one of the coupon formats they offer. These notices state that copayment coupons may not be used to purchase drugs paid for by Federal health care programs, including Medicare Part D. Notices to beneficiaries and pharmacists are more prevalent for print coupons, which is the most commonly offered coupon format according to manufacturers surveyed. Notices are still widely used for other formats, but to a lesser extent. See Table 2 for the percentages of surveyed manufacturers that report using notices for the coupon formats they offer.

Table 2. Notices by Coupon Format

Notice	Print n = 27	Electronic n = 22	Debit Card n = 9	Direct Reimbursement n = 16	Any Format n = 30
Beneficiary Notices	27 (100%)	16 (73%)	8 (89%)	13 (81%)	30 (100%)
Pharmacist Notices	18 (67%)	7 (32%)	2 (22%)	N/A28	20 (67%)

Source: OIG analysis of pharmaceutical manufacturer survey responses, 2013.

Notices Directed to Beneficiaries

Manufacturers' notices directed to beneficiaries are typically printed on coupons or on materials associated with coupons, such as coupon brochures, Web sites, or advertisements. Notices also can be triggered by eligibility questions asked online or over the telephone. Eligibility questions may ask patients: "Do you purchase your prescription medication through Medicare, Medicaid, or a similar Federal or State prescription drug program?" If patients indicate that they are enrolled in Federal health care programs, these manufacturers notify them that they are not eligible to access the coupon.

OIG's review of 40 coupons offered by surveyed manufacturers found results similar to the survey responses. Nearly all of the coupons OIG obtained had a notice printed on them, and 80 percent had a notice printed on the coupon Web site. Further, 75 percent had an eligibility question online or over the phone. However, only 3 percent had a tracking mechanism on their Web sites to prevent a patient from changing his or her answer to the eligibility question to obtain the coupon.

Manufacturers' notices to beneficiaries are typically printed in small font. In some instances, notices are printed on the back of a coupon. See Figure 2 for an example of a coupon with a notice printed in small font on the back. This coupon is approximately the size of a credit card.

In some instances, notices to beneficiaries, particularly those downloaded and printed from the Internet, are on pages following the coupons and not on the coupons themselves. See Figure 3 for an example of a coupon and a notice on the following page. The actual size of each page below is 8 ½ by 11 inches.

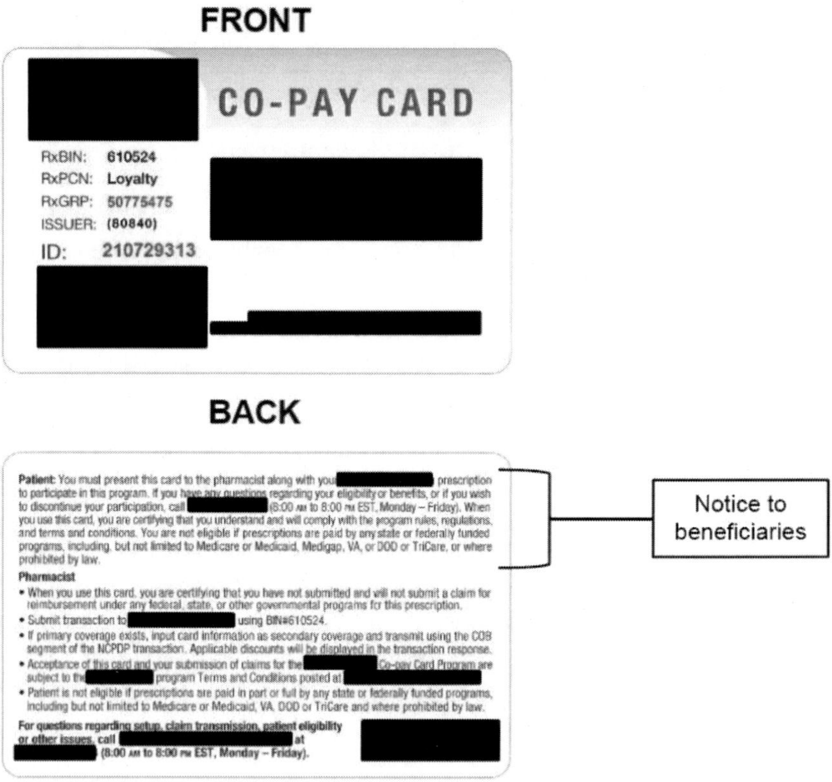

Source: OIG review of manufacturers' copayment coupon safeguards, 2013.

Figure 2. Example of a Coupon with a Notice Printed in Small Font on Back of Coupon.

Notices Directed to Pharmacists

Two-thirds of manufacturers surveyed report providing notices to pharmacists for at least one of the coupon formats they offer. See Table 2, on page 9, for the percentage of survey manufacturers that report using notices to pharmacists broken out by coupon format.

Manufacturers' notices to pharmacists typically include reminders to pharmacists not to accept coupons for drugs paid for by Federal health care programs. These notices may include statements such as "Do not process coupon if Government beneficiary." Or, they may include more specific language, such as "Pharmacist: When you use this card, you are certifying that you have not submitted and will not submit a claim for reimbursement under any Federal, State, or other Governmental programs for this prescription."

Notices to pharmacists can be printed on coupons or on associated materials. They also may appear as alerts to pharmacists through the pharmacy claims transaction system.

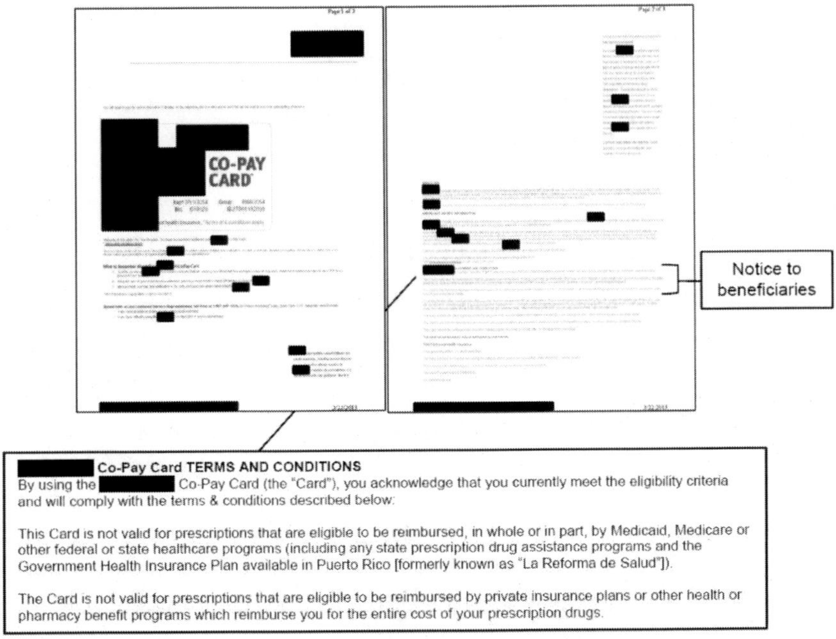

Source: OIG review of manufacturers' copayment coupon safeguards, 2013.

Figure 3. Example of a Coupon With a Notice Printed on Following Page.

OIG's review of the 40 coupons obtained found that slightly more than half, or 58 percent, of coupons we reviewed had notices with specific language directed to pharmacists.

Manufacturers' notices to pharmacists, in some instances, are printed in small font among other types of information, such as instructions on how to process the coupon. See Figure 4 for an example of a coupon with a notice printed among instructions to pharmacists. The actual size of the coupon below is 81/2 by 11 inches.

Additionally, manufacturers' notices may be sent through alert messages within the pharmacy claims transaction system. Studies show that pharmacists may experience "alert fatigue" because of the high volume of drug alert notices that appear through the pharmacy claims transaction system.[29] A notice to check enrollment status in Federal health care programs may be one of the many notices that pharmacists receive.

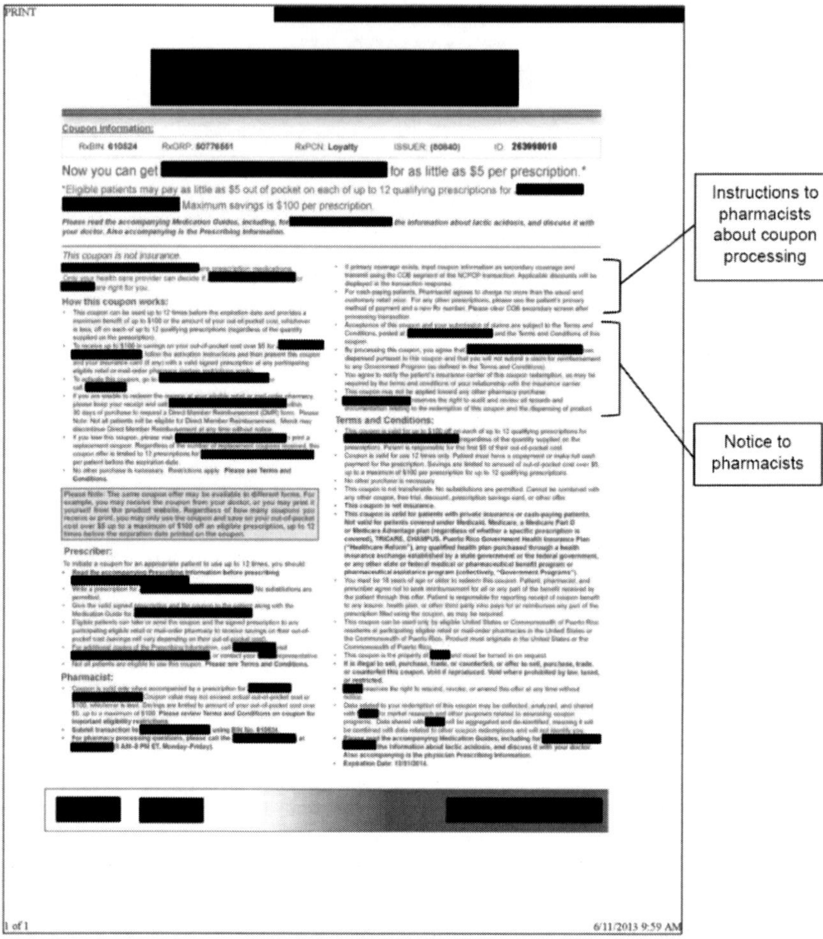

Source: OIG review of manufacturers' copayment coupon safeguards, 2013.

Figure 4. Example of a Coupon With a Notice Printed Among Instructions to Pharmacists.

Manufacturers' notices to beneficiaries and pharmacists only communicate information stipulating the terms and conditions of copayment coupons. These notices cannot necessarily stop coupons from being processed to purchase drugs paid for by Federal health care programs.

Most Surveyed Manufacturers Use Pharmacy Claims Edits to Prevent Copayment Coupons from Being Processed for Drugs Paid for by Part D

Most surveyed manufacturers report having edits in the pharmacy claims transaction system to prevent the use of copayment coupons for drugs paid for by Part D. Twenty-eight of thirty manufacturers surveyed use claims processing edits for at least one of the coupon formats they offer. Of these manufacturers, 13 offered specific information about their edits. More of these manufacturers report using edits for print coupons than for other coupon formats. See Table 3 for information about a breakdown of these edits by coupon formats offered.

Table 3. Claims Processing Edits by Coupon Format

Edit	Print n = 27	Electronic n = 22	Debit Card n = 9	Direct Reimbursement n = 16	Any Format n = 30
Primary Insurance Information	7 (26%)	3 (14%)	1 (11%)	2 (13%)	9 (30%)
Benefit Stage Information	5 (19%)	3 (14%)	0 (0%)	1 (6%)	6 (20%)
Patient Date of Birth	4 (15%)	1 (5%)	0 (0%)	0 (0%)	5 (17%)

Source: OIG analysis of pharmaceutical manufacturer survey responses, 2013.

All of the manufacturers that offered specific information about their claims processing edits use proxies to approximate Part D coverage. The data these manufacturers' edits use as proxies are routinely transmitted on pharmacy claims and include information about a patient's primary insurance, Part D benefit stage, and date of birth. Manufacturers rely on proxies to approximate Part D coverage because they lack access to Part D enrollment status. CMS indicated that Part D enrollment data are not available to manufacturers because they contain sensitive health care information.[30]

Thirty Percent of Manufacturers Use Edits Relying on Primary Insurer's BIN

These manufacturers report having a claims processing edit that uses the primary insurer's BIN for at least one of the coupon formats they offer. The primary insurer's BIN is the only information identifying a patient's primary insurance that is transmitted to manufacturers on the coupon claim. Manufacturers attempt to determine which BINs are used by insurance companies that offer Part D plans by assembling lists of BINs from previously adjudicated primary insurer pharmacy claims and other sources, such as payer sheets.[31] The edit compares the primary insurer's BIN on the coupon claim to the list of collected BINs. If the edit identifies that the primary insurer's BIN represents an insurance company that offers a Part D plan, the claims processing system may automatically stop the coupon from being processed and/or send a message to the pharmacist that the patient is not eligible to use the coupon.

Four surveyed manufacturers report using an edit that relies on the primary insurer's BIN and PCN, the secondary identifier specifying unique insurance plans offered by the same insurance company. The PCN must be obtained from the primary insurance claim because it is not transmitted on the coupon claim. These edits use the BIN and PCN in combination to determine whether the primary insurance claim is being submitted to a Part D plan or a commercial plan within the same insurance company.

Twenty Percent of Manufacturers Use Edits Relying on the Part D Benefit Stage

These manufacturers report having a claims processing edit that uses Part D benefit stage information for at least one of the coupon formats they offer. Benefit stage fields contain data only if the claim is for a Part D beneficiary. If the edit identifies data in these fields, the edit either automatically stops the coupon from being processed or sends a message to the pharmacist to reverse the claim.

Seventeen Percent of Manufacturers Use Edits Relying on Patient Date of Birth

These manufacturers report having an edit that uses the patient's date of birth for at least one of the coupon formats they offer. Manufacturers use edits relying on patient's date of birth to calculate a patient's age. Manufacturers may require pharmacists to submit the patient date of birth as part of the coupon claim. If a pharmacy claim indicates that the patient is at or older than a certain threshold—typically age 62 or 65—these edits will either stop the coupon from being processed or send a message to the pharmacist to verify Part D enrollment.

Surveyed Manufacturers' Pharmacy Claims Edits May Not Prevent Copayment Coupons from Being Processed for Drugs Paid for by Part D

Pharmaceutical manufacturers' claims processing edits currently in use may not stop all coupons from being processed for drugs paid for by Part D because manufacturers cannot accurately identify a beneficiary's Part D enrollment status. Manufacturers' claims processing edits use proxies that are substitutes for but do not replicate actual enrollment information. These proxies use data that may be unreliable or cannot be obtained by all manufacturers.

Claims Processing Edits Using Primary Insurance BINs Cannot Always Accurately Identify Part D Coverage

Manufacturers' claims processing edits that use primary insurers' BINs cannot always identify Part D coverage because they may be unreliable proxies. These edits may not be reliable because they use BIN lists that are collected at a point in time and may not be accurate or current. Further, BINs may not provide the specificity needed to determine whether a patient is enrolled in a Part D plan. Coupon vendors report that the BIN indicates the insurance company but does not, in most cases, distinguish a company's Part D plan from other commercial plans the company offers. To avoid stopping coupon claims associated with commercial plans, manufacturers' BINs lists may contain only BINs known to be exclusively for insurance companies' Part D plans. For instance, one manufacturer reported that its BIN edit relies on a list of BINs dedicated to Part D plans. Thus, this manufacturer's claims processing edit would allow coupons to be processed for claims containing BINs for insurance companies that offer both Part D and commercial plans.

Claims Processing Edits Using Patient Date of Birth Cannot Identify All Part D Beneficiaries

Manufacturer claims processing edits that rely on patient date of birth cannot always approximate Part D coverage. These edits may not identify all Part D beneficiaries because not all Medicare beneficiaries fit a specific age demographic. In fact, 17 percent of Medicare beneficiaries are disabled and under age 65.[32] Additionally, some individuals who are eligible for Medicare may be enrolled in commercial plans and not in Part D.

Some Claims Processing Edits Use More Accurate Proxies To Identify Part D Coverage, but Cannot Be Used by All Manufacturers

Claims processing edits that more accurately determine Part D enrollment are imperfect because these edits use information that cannot be obtained by all manufacturers. These edits rely on the more accurate proxies of BIN/PCN and benefit stage information.

While edits that rely on the primary insurer's BIN/PCN are more accurate proxies, access to this combination of information is limited. To access the BIN/PCN, a manufacturer's coupon vendor needs to have access to primary insurance claims because the PCN is not transmitted as part of the coupon claim. OIG identified one entity with such access to the BIN/PCN. This entity plays a dual role as a coupon vendor and a switching company that electronically routes claims, giving it access to the primary insurance claim containing the BIN/PCN that indicates Part D insurance.

For other manufacturers' coupon vendors to access the PCN, NCPDP would need to revise its pharmacy claims transaction standards to enable the PCN to be transmitted as part of the coupon claim. Revising the NCPDP standards is an industrywide process that typically takes years to complete and requires all involved entities to update their claims transaction systems to comply with the new standards. The current NCPDP standards were updated and released in 2009.

Edits that rely on benefit stage information also are more accurate proxies, but access to this information also is limited. Although some manufacturers report having this edit, it is unclear how they obtain benefit stage information. As cited by NCPDP guidance, only entities that report Part D beneficiaries' financial TrOOP amounts are allowed to request or receive this information, such as insurance companies that offer Part D plans.[33, 34]

Other Vulnerabilities in Claims Processing Edits Exist

In addition to the vulnerabilities associated with the proxies manufacturers use for edits, there may be implementation errors in claims processing edits. Most surveyed manufacturers have no way to verify that edits are being applied correctly because they do not audit claims processing edits. Only 30 percent of manufacturers surveyed report having auditing practices in place to analyze claims processing edits. These audits may include reviews of processes used to identify and reject claims for Part D beneficiaries or retrospective reviews that assess the number of coupons processed and rejected as a result of the edits.

Part D Plans and Other Entities Cannot Identify Copayment Coupons within Pharmacy Claims

It is difficult for entities other than manufacturers to identify coupons as they are processed through the pharmacy claims transaction system or after they are adjudicated. Coupons are not transparent in the pharmacy claims transaction system to entities other than manufacturers. This vulnerability impedes other entities, including Part D plans, other primary insurers, and pharmacies, from preventing the use of coupons for drugs paid for by Part D and oversight entities, like CMS and OIG, from monitoring the use of coupons.

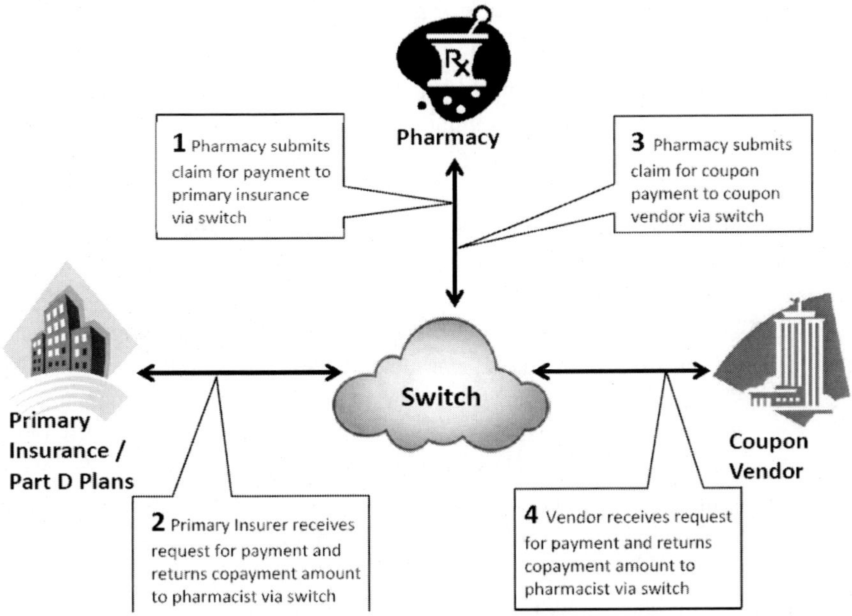

Source: OIG analysis of interview responses, 2013.

Figure 5. Transmission of Information Among Payers and Entities Coordinating Coupon Claims Processing.

Primary insurers, including Part D plans, cannot identify coupons as they are processed or after they are adjudicated because of the way coupons are processed. Coupons are typically processed as secondary insurance claims, after a patient's primary insurance claim, including Part D, has been processed. Because of this, Part D plans, like other primary insurers, cannot identify when a coupon is used. See Figure 5, on the next page, for an illustration of how, as a coupon claim is processed, it is not submitted to primary insurers.

Further, specific coupon formats may be difficult, or impossible, for pharmacists dispensing to beneficiaries on behalf of Part D plans to identify as coupon claims are processed through the pharmacy claims transaction system. When pharmacies cannot identify coupons, they do not know to attempt to verify Part D enrollment to prevent the use of coupons to purchase drugs paid for by Part D. Coupon formats that are difficult to identify include electronic coupons, debit cards, and direct reimbursements. Electronic coupons may be difficult for pharmacists to identify because they are automatically applied as prescriptions are submitted through the pharmacy claims transaction system rather than being presented by patients at the point of sale as with print coupons. Debit card coupons may be difficult to identify because patients may use them to pay their copayments without handing the card to the pharmacist. Finally, direct reimbursements cannot be identified by pharmacists because they are offered directly to patients and processed outside of the pharmacy claims transaction system.

It is also difficult to identify coupons after they are adjudicated. As previously stated, it not always possible to distinguish coupon claims from secondary insurance claims because both manufacturers and insurers use BINs to route claims within the pharmacy claims transaction system. Manufacturers currently do not disclose the BINs associated with their coupons to outside entities. Compiling an accurate and comprehensive list of BINs that route coupon claims without manufacturer involvement would be challenging because coupons expire and BINs, while typically on print coupons, are not generally found on other coupon formats. Because BINs that route coupon claims are not distinguishable from BINs that route insurance claims, entities that conduct oversight, such as CMS and OIG, cannot analyze pharmacy claims to determine whether manufacturer safeguards to prevent the use of coupons for drugs paid for by Part D are effectively stopping the coupons.

CONCLUSION AND RECOMMENDATION

The anti-kickback statute prohibits knowing and willful solicitation, receipt, offer, or payment of remuneration to induce the purchase of any item or service for which payment may be made in whole or in part under a Federal health care program. Pharmaceutical manufacturers may be liable under the anti-kickback statute if they offer coupons to induce the purchase of drugs paid for by Medicare Part D or any other Federal health care program.

Pharmaceutical manufacturers report that they employ safeguards directed at preventing the use of copayment coupons for drugs paid for by Part D. All surveyed manufacturers provide notices to beneficiaries and pharmacists that coupons may not be used in Federal health care programs for at least one of the coupon formats they offer. In addition, most surveyed manufacturers have implemented pharmacy claims edits to prevent coupons from being processed for drugs paid for by Part D.

However, manufacturers' edits may not reliably prevent coupons from being processed for drugs paid for by Part D. In particular, most manufacturers' claims edits only approximate Part D coverage using proxy data that may be unreliable. Additionally, the proxy data that are currently available may not be obtained by all manufacturers.

In addition to potentially implicating the anti-kickback statute, manufacturers' use of coupons to reduce the cost-sharing obligations for drugs paid for by Medicare Part D could impose costs on Part D plans, on the Part D program, and ultimately on Part D beneficiaries. While coupons provide an immediate financial benefit to beneficiaries by reducing their out-of-pocket costs, they may increase the cost of prescription drugs for Part D plans.[35] Coupons may increase costs for Part D plans because they may encourage the purchase of more expensive brand-name drugs instead of less expensive alternative treatments, such as generic drugs.

To protect themselves from excessive costs, Part D plans may have an interest in preventing the use of coupons for drugs paid for by their plans.

However, a lack of coupon transparency impedes Part D plans from distinguishing coupon claims from secondary insurance claims as they are processed. Because entities other than manufacturers cannot identify coupons within pharmacy claims, Part D plans cannot implement their own edits to stop coupon claims as they are processed.

Concurrently with the issuance of this report, OIG is issuing a Special Advisory Bulletin on Pharmaceutical Manufacturer Copayment Coupons. This document affirms that the offerors of coupons ultimately bear the responsibility to operate these programs in compliance with Federal law. Pharmaceutical manufacturers that sponsor copayment coupons may be subject to sanctions if they fail to take appropriate steps to ensure that such coupons do not induce the purchase of Federal health care program items or services, including, but not limited to, drugs paid for by Medicare Part D. Failure to take such steps may be evidence of intent to induce the purchase of drugs paid for by these programs, in violation of the anti-kickback statute.

Improving the reliability of pharmacy claims edits and making coupons transparent within pharmacy claims will likely require the coordination and cooperation of multiple stakeholders within the pharmacy claims transaction process, including CMS. For this reason, pharmaceutical manufacturers may engage industry stakeholders, including CMS, in an effort to identify a solution to ensure that coupons are not used for drugs paid for by Part D.

We recommend that CMS:

Cooperate with Industry Stakeholder Efforts to Identify a Solution to Prevent Coupons from Being Used to Purchase Drugs Paid for by Part D

As the oversight entity of the Part D program and the custodian of Part D enrollment data, CMS should cooperate with industry stakeholder efforts to improve the reliability of pharmacy claims edits and make coupons transparent. For example, CMS could consider all options to facilitate verification of Part D enrollment status before a coupon is processed. Or CMS could explore the possibility of making any feasible changes to the Part D program to facilitate Part D enrollment verification. Additionally, CMS could explore with all involved entities how best to make coupons universally identifiable and transparent in pharmacy claims transactions.

Agency Comments and Office of Inspector General Response

CMS concurred with our recommendation. CMS specifically noted that it concurs with our recommendation to work with relevant stakeholders to improve the reliability of pharmacy claims edits that facilitate verification of Part D enrollment and to explore how best to make coupons universally identifiable and transparent in pharmacy claims data.

For the full text of CMS's comments, see Appendix B.

APPENDIX A

Discussion on Data Collection and Analysis

We collected information about pharmaceutical manufacturer safeguards directed at preventing the use of coupons for drugs paid for by Medicare Part D through a survey of manufacturers and a review of copayment coupon safeguards. We collected information about other vulnerabilities associated with coupon use from interviews with staff at organizations involved in the pharmacy claims processing system.

Drug Selection

We selected the top 100 Part D-covered brand-name drugs by cost that have copayment coupons for the study. These 100 drugs with coupons represent approximately 59 percent of all Part D drug costs.

To select the top 100 Part D-covered brand-name drugs with coupons, we first identified brand-name drugs that were paid for by Part D as of June 2012 using Prescription Drug Event (PDE) data and First DataBank data.36, [37] Using these data, we matched the NDCs for brand-name drugs in First DataBank data to NDCs in PDE data. Because multiple NDCs exist for a single brand-name drug, we collapsed brand-name drugs by the HICL_SEQNO identifier.[38] Next, we summed the total cost for each drug in PDE data by the HICL_SEQNO and the brand name. We then ranked each drug by its total cost.

Next, we compiled a list of 520 coupons from www.internetdrugcoupons.com as of December 2012. Internet Drug Coupons publishes a list of pharmaceutical manufacturer coupons and is recognized by the industry as a reliable listing for coupons.

Finally, we matched the list of coupons to the list of the Part D-covered brand-name drugs. We selected the first 100 Part D-covered brand-name drugs—ranked by total drug cost—with coupons. Because coupons are offered by drug and generally are not unique by package size, dosage form, or route of administration, we matched the common brand name for the drugs associated with these coupons to the brand names and the HICL_SEQNO identifiers in First DataBank.

Survey of Pharmaceutical Manufacturers

In May 2013, we conducted an online survey of the 34 pharmaceutical manufacturers of the top 100 Part D-covered brand-name drugs with copayment coupons.

We identified these manufacturers through information on the coupons and Internet searches. We also asked manufacturers to verify this information. We made one followup attempt by email. We received 30 complete surveys, an 88-percent response rate.

The survey asked manufacturers to provide responses about the safeguards in place for the coupons they offer. We asked manufacturers to report the coupon formats they offer and distribution methods through which patients obtain coupons. We also asked manufacturers about the types of safeguards they have in place for each coupon format they offer. We asked them questions about coupon safeguards directed to Part D beneficiaries, safeguards directed to pharmacists, and safeguards within the pharmacy claims transaction system. We did not ask manufacturers to specify the particular safeguards in place for each of the top 100 Part D-covered brand-name drugs.

We analyzed survey responses to identify specific manufacturer safeguards and determine the extent to which manufacturers surveyed had safeguards in place. For each type of safeguard identified, we calculated the number of manufacturers using the safeguard for at least one of their coupon formats. We also calculated the number of manufacturers with each safeguard by coupon format.

OIG Review of Coupon Safeguards

We reviewed copayment coupon safeguards for a subset of the top 100 Part D-covered brand-name drugs with coupons to determine whether safeguards directed to beneficiaries and pharmacies existed. OIG attempted to obtain 50 coupons, and we reviewed safeguards for the 40 coupons that we obtained. The coupons we attempted to obtain were associated with 24 manufacturers, all of which were included in the population of manufacturers that OIG surveyed. We reviewed coupon safeguards that manufacturers had in place from February to June 2013.

We reviewed and determined the extent to which manufacturers had safeguards directed to beneficiaries on the Internet, over the telephone, and on the print coupons. For safeguards on the Internet and over the telephone, we determined whether: (1) there was a notice about coupon use in Federal health care programs and (2) the notice was triggered by an eligibility question for Part D coverage. For safeguards on the coupons, we determined whether there was a notice directed to beneficiaries about coupon use in Federal health care programs. For each of these safeguards, we calculated the number of manufacturers using it and identified vulnerabilities.

We reviewed and determined the extent to which manufacturers had safeguards directed to pharmacists on the coupons. For these safeguards, we determined whether: (1) there was a general notice on the coupons about coupon use in Federal health care programs and (2) there was a specific notice on the coupons that pharmacists will not submit a claim to a Federal health care program for the prescription with the coupons. We considered a general notice to be any other language directed to pharmacists stating that Federal health care beneficiaries are ineligible to use coupons. We considered a specific notice to be any language that indicates the pharmacist agrees or certifies that he or she will not submit a claim for reimbursement under any Federal health care program or certifies that the patient is not enrolled in any Federal health care program. For each of these safeguards, we calculated the number of manufacturers using the safeguard and identified vulnerabilities.

As part of our review, we attempted to obtain the coupons for which we reviewed safeguards. For coupons available online, we attempted to download coupons and obtained 40 of them. For coupons available over the telephone, we attempted to receive coupons through the mail but obtained none of them.

Structured Interviews

We conducted structured interviews with staff at organizations involved in the pharmacy claims transaction process, including pharmacists, coupon vendors, a switching company, and NCPDP, regarding their experience processing pharmacy claims and coupon claims. We conducted these interviews from February to August 2013. We reviewed structured interview responses to understand other vulnerabilities associated with coupon use. In particular, we discussed the pharmacy claims transaction system and the extent to which coupons are identifiable within it. We also reviewed interview responses to identify vulnerabilities in current safeguards.

APPENDIX B

Agency Comments

DEPARTMENT OF HEALTH & HUMAN SERVICES
Centers for Medicare & Medicaid Services

Administrator
Washington, DC 20201

DATE: JUL 3 0 2014
TO: Daniel R. Levinson
Inspector General
FROM: MatiTyn Tavermer
Administrator

SUBJECT: Office of Inspector General (OIG) Draft Report: "Manufacturer Safeguards May Not Prevent Copayment Coupon Use for Part D Drugs" (OEI-05-12-00540)

The Centers for Medicare & Medicaid Services (CMS) appreciate the opportunity to provide comments on the above mentioned draft report. This draft report assesses the vulnerability of the Part D program to the use of manufacturer's copayment coupons. We are also concerned about the appropriate use of manufacturer's copayment coupons and agree with the OIG that the use of manufacturer's coupons to reduce cost-sharing obligations for drugs paid for by Medicare Part D could impose costs on Part D plans, the Part D program, and ultimately Part D beneficiaries.

OIG Recommendation

The CMS should cooperate with industry stakeholder efforts to identify a solution to prevent coupons from being used to purchase drugs paid for by Part D.

Specifically, the OIG noted that CMS should cooperate with industry stakeholder efforts to improve the reliability of pharmacy claim edits, including considering all options and any feasible changes to the Part D program, to facilitate verification of Part D enrollment status before a coupon is processed. The OIG also suggested that CMS could explore with all involved entities how best to make coupons universally identifiable and transparent in pharmacy claims transactions.

CMS Response

The CMS concurs with the recommendation to work with all relevant stakeholders to find a meaningful solution to prevent inappropriate use of manufacturers' copayment coupons for drugs paid for by Part D. CMS concurs with OIG's suggested recommendation to work with relevant stakeholders to improve the reliability of pharmacy claim edits that facilitate verification of

Part D enrollment and to explore how best to make coupons universally identifiable and transparent in pharmacy claims data.

Thank you for the opportunity to review and comment on the draft OIG report.

ACKNOWLEDGMENTS

This report was prepared under the direction of Ann Maxwell, Regional Inspector General for Evaluation and Inspections in the Chicago regional office, and Laura Kordish, Deputy Regional Inspector General.

Melissa Baker served as the team leader for this study, and Jonathan Jones served as the lead analyst. Central office staff who provided support include Clarence Arnold and Meghan Kearns.

End Notes

[1] Joseph S. Ross and Aaron S. Kesselheim, "Prescription Drug Coupons – No Such Thing as a Free Lunch," *The New England Journal of Medicine*, August 28, 2013, http:// www.nejm.org/doi/pdf/10.1056/NEJMp1301993. Accessed on August 30, 2013. David Grande, "The Cost of Drug Coupons," *JAMA*, June 13, 2012, http://jama. jamanetwork.com/article.aspx?articleid=1182868. Accessed on June 14, 2012. These articles describe how the use of coupons to encourage brand-name drug utilization could increase insurers' costs. This description applies to Medicare Part D, which uses an insurance model to provide prescription drug benefits.

[2] 42 U.S.C. § 1320a-7b(b).

[3] "Federal health care program" is defined in the anti-kickback statute as "(1) any plan or program that provides health benefits, whether directly, through insurance, or otherwise, which is funded directly, in whole or in part, by the United States Government (other than the health insurance program under chapter 89 of title 5; or (2) any State health care program, as defined in section 1320a-7(h) of this title." 42 U.S.C. § 1320a-7b(f).

[4] National Coalition on Health Care (NCHC), "Seniors' Awareness And Use of Prescription Co-pay Coupons in Medicare," Survey. March 26-30, 2012.

[5] Pharmaceutical Care Management Association (PCMA), "Survey of Seniors Enrolled in the Medicare Prescription Drug Plan," Survey. February 15-17, 2011.

[6] Joseph S. Ross and Aaron S. Kesselheim, "Prescription Drug Coupons – No Such Thing as a Free Lunch," *The New England Journal of Medicine*, August 28, 2013, http://www.nejm.org/doi/pdf/10.1056/NEJMp1301993. Accessed on August 30, 2013.

[7] Joseph S. Ross and Aaron S. Kesselheim, "Prescription Drug Coupons – No Such Thing as a Free Lunch," *The New England Journal of Medicine*, August 28, 2013, http://www.nejm.org/doi/pdf/10.1056/NEJMp1301993. Accessed on August 30, 2013. David Grande, "The Cost of Drug Coupons," *JAMA*, June 13, 2012, http://jama.jamanetwork.com/article.aspx?articleid=1182868. Accessed on June 14, 2012.

[8] The Part D program was established as part of the Medicare Prescription Drug, Improvement, and Modernization Act of 2003, P.L. 108-173 § 101; Social Security Act, § 1860D-1 and it was codified at 42 U.S.C. § 1395w-101 et seq.

[9] 42 U.S.C. § 1395w-101 et seq.

[10] Congressional Budget Office, *Effects of Using Generic Drugs on Medicare's Prescription Drug Spending*, September 2010, p. 8.

[11] 42 CFR § 423.104.

[12] *See*, e.g., CMS, Copayment/coinsurance in drug plans, http://www.medicare.gov/part-d/costs/copayment-coinsurance/drug-plan-copayments.html. Accessed on April 24, 2014.

[13] 42 CFR § 423.104(d)(2)(ii).

[14] 42 CFR § 423.120(a)(9).

[15] 42 U.S.C. § 1395w-102(b)(2)(A).

[16] *See*, e.g., CMS, Costs in the coverage gap, http://www.medicare.gov/partd/costs/coverage-gap/part-d-coverage-gap.html. Accessed on April 30, 2014.

[17] 42 U.S.C. § 1395w-114a.

[18] 42 U.S.C. § 1395w-102(b)(2)(C).

[19] For 2013, the TROOP threshold was $4,750. Generally, TrOOP spending includes all beneficiary payments (excluding monthly premiums) and any payments made by other approved payers, such as health savings accounts and certain charities. 42 CFR § 423.104(d)(5)(B)(iii); CMS, *Medicare Prescription Drug Benefit Manual*, Pub. No. 100-18, ch. 5, § 30.

[20] *See*, e.g., CMS, Costs in the coverage gap, http://www.medicare.gov/partd/costs/coverage-gap/part-d-coverage-gap.html. Accessed on April 30, 2014.

[21] *See*, e.g., CMS, Catastrophic coverage, http://www.medicare.gov/partd/costs/catastrophic-coverage/drug-plan-catastrophic-coverage.html. Accessed on May 9, 2014.

[22] Biologics are among the most expensive drugs available. The average cost of a biologic drug is about 22 times that of nonbiologic drugs. "Health Policy Brief: Biosimilars," *Health Affairs*, October 10, 2013, http://healthaffairs.org/healthpolicybriefs/brief_pdfs/healthpolicybrief_100.pdf. Accessed on December 6, 2013.

[23] Cleveland Research Company, "Co-Pay Cards: The Past, Present, and Future," March 2012.

[24] OIG analysis of drugs available on http://www.internetdrugcoupons.com.

[25] OIG analysis of 2009 to 2012 FDA Abbreviated New Drug Approvals (ANDAs) by month available at http://www.accessdata.fda.gov/scripts/cder/drugsatfda/index.cfm?fuseaction=Reports.Re portsMenu.

[26] CMS, *Medicare Prescription Drug Benefit Manual*, Pub. No. 100-18, ch. 14, § 30.4.

[27] CMS, *Changes Involving Medicare Eligibility Queries (E1) and Other TrOOP Facilitator-related Transactions,* December 9, 2010, http://www.cms.gov/Medicare/Prescription-Drug-Coverage/PrescriptionDrugCovContra/Downloads/MemoE1ChangesTipSheet_120910.p df. Accessed on November 30, 2012.

[28] Notices to pharmacists do not pertain to direct reimbursements because direct reimbursements are not adjudicated by the pharmacy.

[29] John R. Horn and Philip D. Hantse, "Making Computerized Screening Work for You," *Pharmacy Times*, February 2006, p. 26.

[30] Because Part D enrollment status is unavailable to manufacturers, those manufacturers that did not offer specific information about their edits likely use proxies and face the same challenges outlined in this report.

[31] Payer sheets are templates created to help claims processors communicate necessary claims processing information to pharmacies, vendors, and other entities. Information on payer sheets can vary by insurance plan but generally contains the BIN.

[32] Henry J. Kaiser Family Foundation, "Medicare at a Glance," November 14, 2012, http://kff.org/medicare/fact-sheet/medicare-at-a-glance-fact-sheet/. Accessed on November 27, 2013.

[33] NCPDP, "NCPDP WG9 Medicare Part D Questions and Answers," Version 3.0, August 2013, p. 12. Accessed at http://www.ncpdp.org/members/wg09/NCPDP_WG9_Medicare_Part_D_FAQ_Documen t_v3.0.pdf on January 30, 2014.

[34] Entities that can obtain benefit stage information may include State pharmaceutical assistance programs.

[35] Manufacturers that desire to assist Federal health care program beneficiaries who cannot afford their copayments have the option of donating to independent charities that provide copayment support without regard for the particular medication a patient may be using. For OIG's guidance specifically related to such charities, see OIG Special Advisory Bulletin on Patient Assistance Programs for Medicare Part D Enrollees, 70 Fed. Reg. 70623 (Nov. 22, 2005), available at http://oig.hhs.gov/fraud/docs/alertsandbulletins/2005/2005PAP Special AdvisoryBulletin.p df, and OIG Supplemental Special Advisory Bulletin: Independent Charity Patient Assistance Programs, available at http://oig.hhs.gov/fraud/docs/alertsandbulletins/2014/independent-charity-bulletin.pdf.

[36] The PDE data represent each purchase of a Part D drug by a beneficiary and contain the National Drug Code (NDC), a universal identifier that specifies the pharmaceutical manufacturer, drug name, dosage form, strength, and package size.

[37] First DataBank data provide product information, including drug name, standard therapeutic class, and whether the drug is a brand-name drug or a generic drug.

[38] The HICL_SEQNO identifies a drug's unique combination of active ingredients, irrespective of the package size, dosage form, route of administration, or strength.

In: Pharmaceutical Industry Developments ISBN: 978-1-63484-649-3
Editor: Kristy Bishop

Chapter 4

PHARMACEUTICAL PATENT-ANTITRUST: REVERSE PAYMENT SETTLEMENTS AND PRODUCT HOPPING*

John R. Thomas

SUMMARY

Congressional attention has recently been directed towards two practices within the pharmaceutical industry. The first pertains to "reverse payment" or "pay-for-delay" settlements of patent litigation. Under this scenario, a generic firm agrees to neither challenge the brand-name company's patents nor sell a generic version of the patented drug for a period of time. In exchange, the brand-name drug company agrees to compensate the generic firm, sometimes with substantial monetary payments over a number of years. Because the payment flows counterintuitively, from the patent owner to the accused infringer, this compensation has been termed a "reverse" payment. Although the private settlement of disputes is usually encouraged, some observers believe that these arrangements are anticompetitive.

Another widely followed practice has been termed "product hopping." Most observers would agree that the introduction of new medicines lies in the public interest. However, some stakeholders have

* This is an edited, reformatted and augmented version of a Congressional Research Service publication R44222, prepared for Members and Committees of Congress, dated October 7, 2015.

accused brand-name firms of releasing new, patent-protected versions of existing drugs—while simultaneously discontinuing an earlier drug that is near patent expiration—with the primary goal of delaying generic entry into the marketplace. Because the Hatch-Waxman Act presupposes the existence of a brand-name drug in order for a generic version to enter the market, product hopping can potentially delay generic competition.

Two notable judicial opinions have subjected these practices to antitrust scrutiny. In its 2013 decision in *Federal Trade Commission v. Actavis, Inc.*, the U.S. Supreme Court held that the legality of reverse payment settlements should be evaluated under the "rule of reason" approach. Under this approach, courts consider whether conduct was reasonable by balancing the anticompetitive consequences of a challenged practice against its business justifications and potentially procompetitive impact. The 2015 decision of the U.S. Court of Appeals for the Second Circuit in *New York ex rel. Schneiderman v. Actavis PLC* applied the rule of reason to product hopping, concluding that this activity may indeed violate the antitrust laws.

Congress possesses a number of alternatives for addressing reverse payment settlements and product hopping. One possibility is to await further judicial developments. Another option is to stipulate antitrust standards that courts and antitrust enforcement agencies would follow in the future. Congress could also alter incentives for generic firms to settle with brand-name firms under the food and drug laws.

INTRODUCTION

The increasing costs of health care have focused congressional attention upon both the development and public availability of prescription drugs. Congress has long recognized that the patent system has an important role to play in the pharmaceutical industry in each respect. The Drug Price Competition and Patent Term Restoration Act of 1984,[1] commonly known as the Hatch-Waxman Act, in part reformed both the patent and food and drug laws in order to balance incentives for innovation and competition within the pharmaceutical industry.[2]

Recently, congressional attention has been directed towards two practices within the pharmaceutical industry. The first pertains to "reverse payment" or "pay-for-delay" settlements of patent litigation. Under this scenario, a generic firm agrees to neither challenge the brand-name company's patents nor sell a generic version of the patented drug for a period of time. In exchange, the brand-name drug company agrees to compensate the generic firm, often with substantial monetary payments over a number of years. Because the payment flows counterintuitively, from the patent owner to the accused infringer, this compensation has been termed a "reverse" payment.[3]

Another widely followed practice has been termed "product hopping." The introduction of new medicines ordinarily serves the public interest. However, some stakeholders have accused brand-name firms of releasing new, patent-protected versions of existing drugs—while simultaneously discontinuing an earlier drug that is near patent expiration—with the primary goal of delaying generic entry into the marketplace. Because the Hatch-Waxman Act presupposes the existence of a brand-name drug in order for a generic version to enter the market, product hopping can potentially delay generic competition. Complaints over product hopping are often accompanied by suspicions over the therapeutic benefits of the newly released drug. But they may raise delicate questions over the competing values of public availability of marginally superior drugs versus lower cost medications.[4]

Two notable judicial opinions have subjected these practices to antitrust scrutiny. In its 2013 decision in *Federal Trade Commission v. Actavis, Inc.*,[5] the U.S. Supreme Court held that the legality of reverse payment settlements should be evaluated under the "rule of reason" approach. Under this approach, courts consider whether conduct was reasonable by balancing the anticompetitive consequences of a challenged practice against its business justifications and potentially procompetitive impact. The 2015 decision of the U.S. Court of Appeals for the Second Circuit in *New York ex rel. Schneiderman v. Actavis PLC*[6] applied the rule of reason to product hopping, concluding that this activity may indeed violate the antitrust laws.

In response to these recent judicial developments, this report introduces and analyzes innovation and competition policy issues associated with the pharmaceutical industry. It begins with a review of the Hatch-Waxman Act and its implications upon the availability of generic substitutes for brand-name medications. The report then turns to a basic review of the antitrust law. It then addresses judicial developments with respect to reverse payment settlements and product hopping. The report closes with a summary of congressional issues and possible alternatives.

THE HATCH-WAXMAN ACT

Patent Fundamentals

Inventors must prepare and submit applications to the U.S. Patent and Trademark Office (USPTO) if they wish to obtain patent protection.[7] USPTO officials, known as examiners, then assess whether the application merits the award of a patent.[8] A patent application must include a specification that so completely describes the invention that skilled artisans are able to practice it without undue experimentation. Applicants must also draft at least one claim that particularly points out and distinctly claims the subject matter that they regard as their invention.[9]

While reviewing a submitted application, the examiner will determine whether the claimed invention fulfills certain substantive standards set by the patent statute. Two of the most important patentability criteria are novelty and nonobviousness. To be judged novel, the claimed invention must not be fully anticipated by a prior patent, publication, or other knowledge within the public domain.[10] The sum of these earlier materials, which document state-of-the-art knowledge that is accessible to the public, is termed the "prior art." To meet the standard of nonobviousness, an invention must not have been readily within the ordinary skills of a competent artisan based upon the teachings of the prior art.[11]

If the USPTO allows the application to issue as a granted patent, the owner or owners of the patent obtain the right to exclude others from making, using, selling, offering to sell, or importing into the United States the claimed invention.[12] The term of the patent is ordinarily set at 20 years from the date the patent application was filed.[13] Patent title therefore provides inventors with limited periods of exclusivity in which they may practice their inventions, or license others to do so. The grant of a patent permits inventors to receive a return on the expenditure of resources leading to the discovery, often by charging a higher price than would prevail in a competitive market. In the pharmaceutical industry, for example, the introduction of generic competition often results in the availability of lower-cost substitutes for the innovative product.

A patent proprietor bears responsibility for monitoring its competitors to determine whether they are using the patented invention. Patent owners who wish to compel others to observe their intellectual property rights must often commence litigation in the federal district courts.

FDA Approval Procedures

Although the award of a patent claiming a pharmaceutical provides its owner with a proprietary interest in that product, it does not actually allow the owner to distribute that product to the public. Permission from the Food and Drug Administration (FDA) must first be obtained.[14] In order to obtain FDA marketing approval, the developer of a new drug must demonstrate that the product is safe and effective. This showing typically requires the drug's sponsor to conduct both preclinical and clinical investigations. In deciding whether to issue marketing approval or not, the FDA evaluates the test data that the sponsor submits in a so-called New Drug Application (NDA).[15]

Prior to the enactment of the Hatch-Waxman Act, the federal food and drug law contained no separate provisions addressing marketing approval for independent generic versions of drugs that had previously been approved by the FDA. The result was that a would-be generic drug manufacturer had to file its own NDA in order to sell its product. Some generic manufacturers could rely on published scientific literature demonstrating the safety and efficacy of the drug by submitting a so-called paper NDA. Because these sorts of studies were not available for all drugs, however, not all generic firms could file a paper NDA. Further, at times the FDA requested additional studies to address safety and efficacy questions that arose from experience with the drug following its initial approval. The result was that some generic manufacturers were forced to prove once more that a particular drug was safe and effective, even though their products were chemically identical to those of previously approved pharmaceuticals.[16]

Some commentators believed that the approval of a generic drug was a needlessly costly, duplicative, and time-consuming process. These observers noted that although patents on important drugs had expired, manufacturers were not moving to introduce generic equivalents for these products due to the level of resource expenditure required to obtain FDA marketing approval.[17]

In response to these concerns, Congress enacted the Hatch-Waxman Act, a complex statute that sought compromise between brand-name and generic pharmaceutical companies.[18] Its provisions included the creation of an expedited marketing approval pathway for generic drugs termed an Abbreviated New Drug Application, or ANDA. An ANDA allows an independent generic applicant to obtain marketing approval by demonstrating that the proposed product is bioequivalent to an approved pioneer drug, without providing evidence of safety and effectiveness from clinical data or from the scientific literature. The availability of ANDAs often allows a generic manufacturer to avoid the costs and delays associated with filing a full-fledged NDA. They may also allow an independent generic manufacturer, in many cases, to place its FDA-approved bioequivalent drug on the market as soon as any relevant patents expire.[19]

As part of the balance struck between brand-name and generic firms, Congress also provided patent proprietors with a means for restoring a portion of the patent term that had been lost while awaiting FDA approval. The maximum extension period is capped at five years, or a total effective patent term after the extension of not more than 14 years. The scope of rights during the period of extension is generally limited to the use approved for the product that subjected it to regulatory delay. This period of patent term extension is intended to compensate brand-name firms for the generic drug industry's reliance upon the proprietary pre-clinical and clinical data they have generated, most often at considerable expense to themselves.[20]

Resolution of Patent Disputes

During its development of accelerated marketing approval procedures for generic drugs, Congress recognized that the brand-name pharmaceutical firm may be the proprietor of one or more patents directed towards that drug product. These patents might be infringed by a product described by a generic firm's ANDA or in the event that product is approved by the FDA and sold in the marketplace. The Hatch-Waxman Act therefore established special procedures for resolving patent disputes in connection with applications for marketing generic drugs.[21]

In particular, the Hatch-Waxman Act states that each NDA applicant "shall file" a list of patents that the applicant believes would be infringed if a generic drug were marketed prior to the expiration of these patents.[22] The FDA then lists these patents in a publication titled *Approved Drug Products with Therapeutic Equivalence Evaluations*, which is more commonly known as the "Orange Book."[23] Would-be manufacturers of generic drugs must then engage in a specialized certification procedure with respect to Orange Book-listed patents. An ANDA applicant must state its views with respect to each Orange Book-listed patent associated with the drug it seeks to market. Four possibilities exist:

(1) that the brand-name firm has not filed any patent information with respect to that drug;

(2) that the patent has already expired;
(3) that the generic company agrees not to market until the date on which the patent will expire; or
(4) that the patent is invalid or will not be infringed by the manufacture, use, or sale of the drug for which the ANDA is submitted.[24]

These certifications are respectively termed paragraph I, II, III, and IV certifications. An ANDA certified under paragraphs I or II is approved immediately after meeting all applicable regulatory and scientific requirements. An independent generic firm that files an ANDA including a paragraph III certification must, even after meeting pertinent regulatory and scientific requirements, wait for approval until the drug's listed patent expires.[25]

The filing of an ANDA with a paragraph IV certification constitutes a "somewhat artificial" act of patent infringement under the Hatch-Waxman Act.[26] The act requires the independent generic applicant to notify the proprietor of the patents that are the subject of a paragraph IV certification. The patent owner may then commence patent infringement litigation against that applicant.[27]

In order to encourage challenges of pharmaceutical patents, the Hatch-Waxman Act provides prospective manufacturers of generic pharmaceuticals with a potential reward. That reward consists of a 180-day exclusivity period awarded to the first ANDA applicant to file a paragraph IV certification.[28] Once a first ANDA with a paragraph IV certification has been filed, the FDA cannot issue marketing approval to a subsequent ANDA with a paragraph IV certification on the same drug product for 180 days. Because market prices could drop considerably following the entry of additional generic competition, the first paragraph IV ANDA applicant may potentially obtain more handsome profits than subsequent market entrants—thereby stimulating patent challenges in the first instance.[29]

ANTITRUST FUNDAMENTALS

The primary legal mechanism for addressing conduct alleged to be anticompetitive—including reverse payment settlements and product hopping—consists of the antitrust laws. The antitrust laws consist of the Sherman Act, the Clayton Act, the Federal Trade Commission Act, and other federal and state statutes that prohibit certain kinds of anticompetitive economic conduct.

Although a complete review of the antitrust laws exceeds the scope of this report, other sources provide more information for the interested reader.[30]

Section 1 of the Sherman Act declares "[e]very contract, combination in the form of trust or otherwise, or conspiracy, in restraint of trade ... to be illegal." The courts have long interpreted this language as applying only to unreasonable restraints of trade. The determination of whether particular conduct amounts to an unreasonable restraint of trade is commonly conducted under the "rule of reason." Under this approach, "the finder of fact must decide whether the questioned practice imposes an unreasonable restraint on competition, taking into account a variety of factors, including specific information about the relevant business, its condition before and after the restraint was imposed, and the restraint's history, nature, and effect."[31] The rule of reason essentially calls upon courts to reach a judgment of reasonableness by balancing the anticompetitive consequences of a challenged practice against its business justifications and potentially procompetitive impact.[32]

Other sorts of restraints are deemed unlawful *per se*. *Per se* illegality is appropriate "[o]nce experience with a particular kind of restraint enables the Court to predict with confidence that the rule of reason will condemn it." The Supreme Court has explained that "there are certain agreements or practices which because of their pernicious effect on competition and lack of any redeeming virtue are conclusively presumed to be unreasonable and therefore illegal without elaborate inquiry as to the precise harm they have caused or the business excuse for their use."[33] Among the practices that have been judged per se violations include price fixing, group boycotts, and market division.[34]

In some circumstances, courts apply an antitrust standard that falls between the *per se* illegality standard and the rule of reason. The so-called "quick look" or "truncated rule of reason" approach applies when the plaintiff demonstrates that the defendant has engaged in practices similar to those previously held to be subject to *per se* treatment. In these circumstances, the defendant must then demonstrate that the practice has pro-competitive justifications in order to avoid liability for an antitrust violation.[35]

Reverse Payment Settlements

As discussed previously, a generic firm's filing of a paragraph IV ANDA may result in a patent infringement suit brought by a brand-name drug company. In such litigation, if the NDA holder demonstrates that the independent generic firm's proposed product would violate its patents, then the court will ordinarily issue an injunction that prevents the generic drug company from marketing that product. That injunction will expire on the same date as the NDA holder's patents. Independent generic drug companies commonly amend their ANDAs in this event, replacing their paragraph IV certifications with paragraph III certifications.[36]

On the other hand, the courts may decide in favor of the independent generic firm. The court may conclude that the generic firm's proposed product does not infringe the asserted patents, or that the asserted patents are invalid or unenforceable. In this circumstance, the independent generic firm may launch its product once the FDA has finally approved its ANDA.[37]

In addition to the issuance of final judgment in favor of either the brand-name drug company or generic firm, another resolution of pharmaceutical patent litigation is possible. This legal situation led to a number of cases with varying details, but a common core fact pattern. Upon filing a paragraph IV ANDA, a generic firm would be sued for patent infringement as provided by the Hatch-Waxman Act. The NDA holder and generic applicant would then settle their dispute. The settlement would call for the generic firm to neither challenge the patent nor produce a generic version of the patented drug, for a period of time up to the remaining term of the patent. In exchange, the NDA holder would agree to compensate the ANDA applicant, often with substantial monetary payments over a number of years.[38] This compensation has been termed an "exclusion"[39] or "exit"[40] payment or, because the payment flows counterintuitively, from the patent proprietor to the accused infringer, a "reverse" payment.[41]

Notice of Payment Settlements

Congress initially addressed reverse payment settlements in 2003 with the Medicare Prescription Drug, Improvement, and Modernization Act (MMA).[42] That legislation mandated that the Department of Justice (DOJ) and Federal Trade Commission (FTC) receive copies of certain patent- or exclusivity-based settlement agreements in the pharmaceutical field. Section 1112 of the MMA sets out two sorts of agreements that are subject to this notice requirement: Section 1112(a) agreements between a brand-name drug company and a paragraph IV ANDA applicant, and Section 1112(b) agreements between two paragraph IV ANDA applicants.

Section 1112(a) agreements must occur between an ANDA applicant, on one hand, and either the NDA holder or an owner of an Orange Book-listed patent, on the other.[43] Such agreements are subject to the MMA's notification requirement if their subject matter relates to one of three topics:

(1) The manufacture, marketing, or sale of the brand-name drug that is listed in the ANDA;
(2) The manufacture, marketing, or sale of the generic drug for which the ANDA was submitted; or
(3) The 180-day generic exclusivity period[44] as it applies to that ANDA, or to another ANDA filed with respect to the same brand-name drug.[45]

In turn, Section 1112(b) requires that agreements between two paragraph IV ANDA applicants relating to the 180-day generic exclusivity provision be submitted to the DOJ and FTC.[46]

The MMA stipulates that certain agreements are not subject to this filing requirement. In particular, agreements that solely consist of purchase orders for raw materials, equipment and facility contracts, employment or consulting contracts, or packaging and labeling contracts need not be submitted to the DOJ or FTC.[47] Failure to file in keeping with MMA requirements exposes a contracting party to a civil penalty, compliance order, and other equitable relief.[48]

FTC v. Actavis

Although the MMA required pharmaceutical firms to inform the government concerning reverse payment settlements, that legislation did not impose substantive standards concerning antitrust oversight of these arrangements.[49] The courts were left to develop the appropriate level of antitrust oversight of these settlements. Facing somewhat different facts, they developed varying approaches to the issue.[50] However, these distinctions were laid to rest by the 2013 Supreme Court opinion in *Federal Trade Commission v. Actavis, Inc.*[51]

In *Actavis*, the Supreme Court held that the legality of reverse payment settlements should be evaluated under the "rule of reason" approach.[52] However, the Court declined to hold that such settlements should be presumptively illegal under a "quick look" analysis.[53] The *Actavis* opinion resolves a longstanding split among the lower courts regarding the approach that should be taken toward settlement of pharmaceutical patent cases under the antitrust laws. The lower courts now face the potentially complex task of applying the rule of reason to reverse payment settlements going forward.[54]

The patent proprietor in the *Actavis* litigation was Solvay Pharmaceuticals, the NDA holder of the testosterone-replacement drug Andro Gel. When generic firms Actavis and Paddock Laboratories filed paragraph IV ANDAs, Solvay brought charges of patent infringement in keeping with the Hatch-Waxman Act. The parties ultimately settled the case, with the generic firms receiving cash payments in exchange for the promise not to market their products until August 31, 2015, 65 months before Solvay's patent expired.[55]

The FTC subsequently charged the settling parties with a violation of section 5 of the Federal Trade Commission Act,[56] in that they unlawfully agreed "to share in Solvay's monopoly profits, abandon their patent challenges, and refrain from launching their low-cost generic products to compete with AndroGel for nine years."[57] The District Court for the Northern District of Georgia rejected the FTC's claims,[58] and on appeal the Eleventh Circuit affirmed. Applying the "scope of the patent" standard that had been developed in earlier cases, the Court of Appeals explained that "absent sham litigation or fraud in obtaining a patent, a reverse payment settlement is immune from antitrust attack so long as its anticompetitive effects fall within the exclusionary potential of the patent."[59]

The Supreme Court subsequently agreed to hear the case. In a 5-3 ruling, the Supreme Court reversed the judgment of the Eleventh Circuit and remanded. Writing for the majority, Justice Breyer accepted that the anticompetitive effects of the agreement between Solvay and the generic firms fell with the scope of its patent. However, this fact by itself did not immunize the agreement from antitrust scrutiny. The majority explained that while the holder of a valid patent may be exempt from antitrust liability when enforcing the exclusionary right, litigation under the Hatch-Waxman Act involves assertions of patent invalidity or noninfringement. If the generic firm successfully makes either case, the patent proprietor would not enjoy the right to exclude the proposed generic product from the marketplace. As a result, such agreements may have significant adverse effects on competition.

Justice Breyer therefore reasoned that "it would be incongruous to determine antitrust legality by measuring the settlement's anticompetitive effects solely against patent law policy, rather than by measuring them against procompetitive antitrust policies as well."[60] Observing that its precedent had held that certain patent-related settlements can violate the antitrust laws, the Court summarized its patent-antitrust case law as follows:

> [R]ather than measure the length or amount of a restriction solely against the length of the patent's term or its earning potential, as the Court of Appeals apparently did here, this Court answered the antitrust question by considering traditional antitrust factors such as likely anticompetitive effects, redeeming virtues, market power, and potentially offsetting legal considerations present in the circumstances, such as here those related to patents.[61]

The Court also concluded that the structure of the Hatch-Waxman Act—including its patent challenge provisions, requirement of notification of settlements to the antitrust authorities, and its "general procompetitive thrust"—was consistent with subjecting reverse payment settlements to antitrust scrutiny.[62]

Justice Breyer acknowledged that the strong judicial policy favoring the settlement of disputes supported the holding of the Eleventh Circuit. But he cited five considerations in support of a contrary result:

> [A] reverse payment, where large and unjustified, can bring with it the risk of significant anticompetitive effects; one who makes such a payment may be unable to explain and to justify it; such a firm or individual may well possess market power derived from the patent; a court, by examining the size of the payment, may well be able to assess its likely anticompetitive effects along with its potential justifications without litigating the validity of the patent; and parties may well find ways to settle patent disputes without the use of reverse payments. In our view, these considerations, taken together, outweigh the single strong consideration—the desirability of settlements—that led the Eleventh Circuit to provide near-automatic antitrust immunity to reverse payment settlements.[63]

Finally, Justice Breyer declined to adopt the Commission's suggestion that reverse payment settlements should be presumptively unlawful and subject to a "quick-look approach." According to the majority, this approach was appropriate only where "an observer with even a rudimentary understanding of economics could conclude that the arrangements in question would have an anticompetitive effect on customers and markets."[64] This treatment was inappropriate in this case because the likelihood of a reverse payment bringing about anticompetitive effects depends upon a number of factors, including the size of the payment, its scale in relation to the payor's anticipated litigation costs, its independence from other consideration within the settlement, and the lack of any other convincing justification. Instead, the Court concluded that the FTC must establish antitrust liability using the traditional rule of reason analysis.[65]

Chief Justice Roberts contributed a dissent that was joined by Justices Scalia and Thomas. The dissenters would have held that a reverse payment settlement violates antitrust law only when it exceeds the scope of the patent, the patents were obtained by fraud, or the patentee engages in sham litigation.[66] The dissenters feared that the majority holding would dissuade generic firms from challenging patents in the first place,[67] discourage settlement of patent litigation,[68] and weaken the protection afforded to innovators by patents.[69]

Commentators have viewed the ruling in *Actavis* as making a significant change to patent-antitrust practice. Although the Supreme Court's opinion does not eliminate the ability of pharmaceutical firms to settle litigation under the Hatch-Waxman Act, the contracting parties will have to structure and explain their agreements with greater care. Parties may also be more willing to litigate their pharmaceutical patent cases to a final conclusion. With respect to existing agreements, the lower courts have been assigned the potentially complex task of giving substance to the rule of reason in Hatch-Waxman cases.

Post-Actavis Developments

Although commentators initially expected that reverse payment settlements would be subject to more severe antitrust scrutiny in the future,[70] several district court opinions issued shortly after *Actavis* continued to uphold the settlements as lawful.[71] However, as suggested by the 2015 decision of the U.S. Court of Appeals for the Third Circuit in *King Drug Co. of Florence, Inc. v. Smithkline Beecham Corp.*,[72] lower court response to *Actavis* continues to evolve. *King Drug v. Smithkline Beecham* addressed two important issues: (1) whether the *Actavis* holding was limited to cash payments, as compared to other forms of contractual consideration; and (2) whether *Actavis* dictated the substantive terms of the rule of reason analysis the lower courts were meant to apply.

As to the first issue, reverse payment settlements have often involved a cash payment made by the brand-name firm to the generic firm. However, the facts of litigated cases reveal that many such settlements have involved non-cash consideration instead. Possible non-cash consideration includes payment for unrelated generic services, such as backup manufacturing capacity or the promise to supply a raw material used to make the pharmaceutical.[73]

Shortly after the Supreme Court issued *Actavis*, at least two district courts held that its ruling was limited to settlements where the brand-name firm paid cash to the generic firm.[74] These courts observed that the *Actavis* opinion frequently focused upon the form of consideration that was relevant to that case, namely, cash. They further concluded that the rule of reason analysis compelled by *Actavis* could reasonably be accomplished with respect to a cash payment. However, non-cash consideration was deemed to be difficult to quantify numerically. As a result, these courts limited *Actavis* to its specific facts and upheld settlements that did not involve the transfer of cash.

However, the U.S. Court of Appeals for the Third Circuit rejected this analysis in *King Drug v. Smithkline Beecham.*[75] Writing for the Court of Appeals, Judge Scirica concluded that non-cash agreements potentially transferred considerable wealth from the brand-name firm to the generic firm.[76] Judge Scirica also explained that simply because the patent laws generally allow patent proprietors to license their patents does not immunize a particular license with anticompetitive effects from antitrust scrutiny.[77] Rejecting the argument that the Supreme Court intended to draw a formal line between cash and non-cash consideration in *Actavis*, the Third Circuit held that an unusual, unexplained transfer of value from the patent proprietor to the alleged infringer is subject to the rule of reason.[78]

Judge Scirica's reasoning in *King Drug* potentially applies to any transfer of value between parties settling a patent case. Because brand-name firms are typically uninterested in obtaining the services of generic firms outside the context of a patent settlement, *King Drug v. Smithkline Beecham* considerably buttresses the *Actavis* ruling and extends its logic to a wide swath of commercial arrangements. Whether the other courts of appeal will adopt the logic of the Third Circuit remains to be seen.

Some disagreement among commentators has also arisen about the substantive scope of the rule of reason analysis. A staple of antitrust law, the rule of reason analysis requires courts to consider whether the parties to the reverse payment settlement had market power and exercised it, whether the restraint had anti-competitive consequences, and whether these consequences are otherwise justified.[79] In an attempt to apply these basic principles within the context of reverse payments settlements, certain lower courts made considerable use of the "five sets of considerations" on which Justice Breyer relied to overcome the strong judicial preference for private settlement of disputes. In particular, Justice Breyer explained that "a reverse payment, where large and unjustified, can bring with it the risk of significant anticompetitive effects; one who makes such a payment may be unable to explain and to justify it; such a firm or individual may well possess market power derived from the patent; a court, by examining the size of the payment, may well be able to assess its likely anticompetitive effects along with its potential justifications without litigating the validity of the patent; and parties may well find ways to settle patent disputes without the use of reverse payments."[80]

Most readers of the *Actavis* opinion viewed these five factors as expressing the Supreme Court's rationales for adopting a rule of reason approach for analyzing the antitrust implications of reverse payment settlements. However, some district courts instead believed these factors were intended "to guide district courts in applying the rule of reason in this context.... "[81] Put differently, factors that the Supreme Court seemingly provided as a justification for its holding were viewed as defining standards for conducting the rule of reason analysis itself. Under this approach, the lower courts would essentially analyze whether a particular reverse payment settlement should be governed by the rule of reason on a case-by-case basis. However, the Supreme Court already concluded that they should, and therefore this sort of analysis is unnecessary.

The U.S. Court of Appeals for the Third Circuit recognized this problem and attempted to restore order to the rule of reason analysis in *King Drug v. Smithkline Beecham*.[82] The Third Circuit there explained that district courts should not view the five justifications that the Supreme Court offered in *Actavis* as an expression of the rule of reason itself. Rather, the district courts should proceed immediately to the rule of reason analysis when reviewing reverse payment settlements. This reading of *Actavis* will prevent courts from imposing a more difficult burden upon antitrust plaintiffs in reverse payment settlement cases than in other categories of litigation.

PRODUCT HOPPING

Congress intended both the patent laws, on one hand, and the food and drug laws, on the other, to promote the development of new drugs. FDA approval of a new medication would therefore appear to promote the public interest. Antitrust enforcers have become increasingly concerned, however, that new drugs may be developed and marketed for the principal purpose of delaying generic entry. In particular, some stakeholders have accused brand-name drug companies of introducing new, patented drugs while contemporaneously removing off-patent drugs from the marketplace. This practice has been termed "product hopping," at least by its detractors.[83]

The reasons that product hopping deters generic competition are more subtle than may first appear.[84] Merely because a brand-name firm withdraws its products from the market, accompanied by removal of the drug from the Orange Book, would not prevent a generic firm from filing an ANDA rather than an NDA. The FDA has expressly concluded that an ANDA "that refers to ... a listed drug that has been voluntarily withdrawn from sale in the United States must be accompanied by a petition seeking a determination whether the listed drug was withdrawn for safety or effectiveness reasons."[85] Put differently, an ANDA applicant need only demonstrate that a withdrawn reference product was not removed from the market for safety or effectiveness reasons in order to obtain marketing approval.

The principal reason that product hopping is a potentially effective generic exclusion strategy has more to do with state drug substitution laws. Under the laws of all 50 states and the District of Columbia, pharmacists are either permitted or required to dispense a therapeutically equivalent generic drug in place of a brand-name drug unless the prescribing physician has stipulated otherwise. Most states and the District of Columbia have adopted the FDA's definition of "therapeutically equivalent"—namely, a generic drug must be designated as "AB"-rated within the Orange Book to be deemed therapeutically equivalent to a brand-name drug.[86] Generic drug companies commonly compete with brand-name firms through state drug substitution laws. As a result of this situation, when a brand-name firm "product hops" by withdrawing an off-patent drug and introducing a new, patented medication, generic firms may not be deemed therapeutically equivalent to the new drug under state law and therefore will not be substituted for brand-name prescriptions.[87]

Until 2015, judicial precedent addressing product hopping was sparse and limited to decisions of the federal district courts.[88] The watershed decision of the U.S. Court of Appeals for the Second Circuit in *New York ex rel. Schneiderman v. Actavis PLC*[89] considerably altered the judicial landscape, providing that product hopping may indeed violate the antitrust laws. For sake of clarity, this report will refer to the Second Circuit's effort as the *Namenda* decision. Issued two years after the Supreme Court groundbreaking decision in

Actavis, the *Namenda* opinion will likely embolden both government enforcers and the private plaintiffs' bar to pursue additional product hopping cases.

Namenda involved two versions of the Alzheimer's drug, Namenda IR and Namenda XR. Namenda IR is a twice-daily drug that neared the end of patent protection during July 2015. As a result, Actavis introduced a new, once-daily extended release version called Namenda XR. According to the Attorney General of New York, Actavis initially embarked upon a "soft switch" strategy by continuing to market both drugs but actively promoting Namenda XR. By early 2014, Actavis shifted to a "hard switch" approach by notifying the FDA it would discontinue Namenda IR, with one limited exception. Actavis also requested that the Centers for Medicare and Medicaid Services remove Namenda IR from their formularies, with the result that Medicare health plans would not cover it.[90]

The New York Attorney General responded by bringing an antitrust suit against Actavis, asserting that it had violated state and federal antitrust laws. The U.S. District Court for the Southern District of New York issued a preliminary injunction requiring that Actavis continue to market Namenda IR until 30 days after July 11, 2015, the date of generic entry.[91] Actavis then appealed to the Second Circuit, which affirmed the grant of the injunction.

Writing for a three-judge panel, Judge Walker acknowledged that innovation generally benefits consumers.[92] However, he concluded that the Namenda product hop was both anticompetitive and exclusionary. In particular, the Second Circuit found that Actavis had crossed the line from permissible "soft switch" persuasion to impermissible "hard switch" coercion. The Court of Appeals also believed that the removal of Namenda IR would substantially reduce competition. Judge Walker found that withdrawal of Namenda IR would necessarily convert patients to Namenda XR with little probability of their switching back to Namenda IR once a generic version became available.[93]

Judge Walker also found little evidence of procompetitive justifications for withdrawing Namenda IR from the market. He cited evidence that Actavis intended to delay generic competition and further found no evidence that antitrust scrutiny would meaningfully deter innovation.[94] The Second Circuit concluded "that the combination of withdrawing a successful drug [IR] from the market and introducing a reformulated version of that drug [XR], which has the dual effect of forcing patients to switch to the new version and impeding generic competition, without a legitimate business justification, violates §2 of the Sherman Act."[95]

The *Namenda* decision leaves open a number of issues that future litigation might resolve. First, the Second Circuit seems to imply that a "soft switch" approach of aggressive marketing, but maintaining the older product on the market, would not run afoul of the antitrust laws. The sorts of activities that, in the words of the Court of Appeals, "crosses the line" to impermissible conduct remains to be seen. Second, many critics of product hopping have suggested that newly introduced products do not provide much of an improvement over the old. In circumstances where the new medicine is superior to its predecessor, perhaps the courts will prove more sympathetic to product hopping. Finally, the extent to which brand-name firms must actively support their generic competitors by keeping older products on the market may prove a divisive issue.

ISSUES AND OBSERVATIONS

In the absence of explicit congressional guidance, the federal courts have applied general principles of antitrust law to address reverse payment settlements and product hopping. Several options are available for Congress. One possibility is to await further judicial developments in view of the *Actavis* and *Namenda* decisions.

Another option is to regulate the settlement of pharmaceutical patent litigation in some manner. In the 114th Congress, the Fair and Immediate Release of Generics Act (S. 131), introduced by Senator Bingaman, would make a number of changes to the Hatch-Waxman Act in order to discourage reverse payments settlements. In particular, S. 131 would grant any generic firm the right to share the 180-day regulatory exclusivity if it wins a patent challenge in the district court or is not sued for patent infringement by the brand company.[96] The legislation would also oblige generic firms to abide by any deferred entry date agreed to in their settlements with brand-name firms, even if relevant patents were struck down previously.[97] Finally, brand-name firms would be required to make a decision to enforce their patents within 45 days of being notified of a patent challenge by a generic firm under the Hatch-Waxman Act.[98]

In addition, the Preserve Access to Affordable Generics Act (S. 2019), introduced by Senator Klobuchar, would declare that certain reverse payment settlements constitute acts of unfair competition. In particular, that bill would amend the Federal Trade Commission Act to provide that an agreement "shall be presumed to have anticompetitive effects and be unlawful if—(i) an ANDA filer receives anything of value; and (ii) the ANDA filer agrees to limit or forego research, development, manufacturing, marketing, or sales of the ANDA product for any period of time." Certain exceptions apply—for example, the payment of reasonable litigation expenses not exceeding $7.5 million is not unlawful. That "quick look" presumption would not apply if the parties to the agreement demonstrated by clear and convincing evidence that the procompetitive benefits of the agreement outweighed the anticompetitive effects of the agreement. S. 2019 includes a list of factors to be weighed by the courts in such circumstances.[99]

A third bill, S. 2023, the Prescription Drug Affordability Act of 2015, was introduced by Senator Sanders. Title IV of this legislation would act similarly to S. 2019. It would also create a presumption that reverse payment settlements violated the Federal Trade Commission Act, subject to certain exceptions. However, unlike S. 2019, the parties to the agreement cannot overcome this presumption by showing that its procompetitive benefits outweighed the anticompetitive harms.

Congress has yet to consider legislation with respect to product hopping. If the current situation is deemed satisfactory, then no action need be taken. Another alternative is to encourage more active antitrust enforcement in this area in view of the *Namenda* decision. And although the rules governing generic substitution are currently a matter of state law, federal oversight of these principles could also discourage product hopping.

The interaction between brand-name and generic firms forms an important component of the public health system of the United States. The U.S. patient population relies upon brand-name drug companies to develop new medicines, but it also relies upon generic firms to increase access to such medications once they have been developed. The Hatch-Waxman Act provides for patent litigation between these two traditional rivals, as well as generic substitution, as the mechanisms through which these competing demands are mediated. When concluded in a manner that comports with antitrust principles, these practices may further the public policy goals of encouraging the labors that lead to medical innovation, but also distributing the fruits of those labors to consumers.

End Notes

[1] P.L. 98-417, 98 Stat. 1585.

[2] CRS Report R41114, The Hatch-Waxman Act: Over a Quarter Century Later, by Wendy H. Schacht and John R. Thomas.

[3] See, e.g., Michael A. Carrier, "After Actavis: Seven Ways Forward," 67 Rutgers University Law Review 543 (2015).

[4] See, e.g, Lars Noah, "Product Hopping 2.0: Getting the FDA to Yank Your Original License Beats Stacking Patents," 19 Marquette Intellectual Property Law Review 161 (2015).

[5] 133 S. Ct. 2223 (2013).

[6] 787 F.3d 638 (2d Cir. 2015).

[7] 35 U.S.C. §111.

[8] 35 U.S.C. §131.

[9] 35 U.S.C. §112.

[10] 35 U.S.C. §101.

[11] 35 U.S.C. §103.

[12] 35 U.S.C. §271.

[13] 35 U.S.C. §154(a)(2).

[14] CRS Report R41983, How FDA Approves Drugs and Regulates Their Safety and Effectiveness, by Susan Thaul.

[15] See FDA, "Drugs: Development and Approval Process (Drugs): How Drugs Are Developed and Approved," April 23, 2010 (available at http://www.fda.gov/drugs/development approvalprocess/howdrugsaredevelopedandapproved/default.htm).

[16] See Colleen Kelly, "The Balance Between Innovation and Competition: The Hatch-Waxman Act, the 2003 Amendments, and Beyond," 66 Food and Drug Law Journal (2011), 417.

[17] See Matthew Avery, "Continuing Abuse of the Hatch-Waxman Act by Pharmaceutical Patent Holders and the Failure of the 2003 Amendments," 60 Hastings Law Journal (2008), 171.

[18] See Timothy A. Cook, "Pharmaceutical Patent Litigation Settlements: Balancing Patent and Antitrust Policy Through Institutional Choice," 17 Michigan Telecommunications and Technology Law Review (2011), 417.

[19] See Michael R. Herman, "The Stay Dilemma: Examining Brand and Generic Incentives for Delaying the Resolution of Pharmaceutical Patent Litigation," 111 Columbia Law Review (2011), 1788.

[20] See Ann Kotze, "Reining in Patent Term Extensions for Related Pharmaceutical Products Post-Photocure and OrthoMcNeil," 106 Northwestern University Law Review (2012), 1419.

[21] See Linda P. Nussbaum and John D. Radice, "Where Do We Go Now? The Hatch-Waxman Act Twenty-Five Years Later: Successes, Failures, and Prescriptions for the Future," 41 Rutgers Law Journal (2009), 229.

[22] 21 U.S.C. §355(b)(1).

[23] See Ian Hastings, "Dynamic Innovation Inefficiency in Pharmaceutical Patent Settlements," 13 North Carolina Journal of Law and Technology (2011), 31.

[24] 21 U.S.C. §355(j)(2)(A)(vii).

[25] See Emily Michiko Morris, "The Myth of Generic Pharmaceutical Competition Under the Hatch-Waxman Act," 22 Fordham Intellectual Property Media and Entertainment Law Journal (2012), 245.

[26] Eli Lilly & Co. v. Medtronic, 496 U.S. 1047 (1990).

[27] See Morris, supra.

[28] 21 U.S.C. §355(j)(5)(B)(iv).

[29] See Scott Hemphill and Mark A. Lemley, "Earning Exclusivity: Generic Drug Incentives and the Hatch-Waxman Act," 77 Antitrust Law Review (2011), 947.

[30] See, e.g., Federal Trade Commission, FTC Guide to the Antitrust Laws (available at http://www.ftc.gov/bc/antitrust/).

[31] State Oil Co. v. Khan, 522 U.S. 3, 10 (1997).

[32] See Meredith Bateman, "In re K-Dur Antitrust Litigation—Reverse Payments: Against Prices, Purchasers, and Policy," 15 Tulane Journal of Technology and Intellectual Property (2012), 293.

[33] Northern Pacific Railroad Co. v. United States, 356 U.S. 1, 5 (1957).

[34] See Leegin Creative Leather Products, Inc. v. PSKS, Inc., 551 U.S. 877 (2007).

[35] See California Dental Association v. FTC, 526 U.S. 756 (1999).

[36] 21 C.F.R. §314.94(a)(12)(viii)(A).

[37] 21 U.S.C. §355(j)(5)(B)(iii).

[38] See C. Scott Hemphill, "Paying for Delay: Pharmaceutical Patent Settlement as a Regulatory Design Problem," 81 New York University Law Review (2006), 1560.

[39] See Herbert Hovenkamp et al., "Balancing Ease and Accuracy in Assessing Pharmaceutical Exclusion Payments," 88 Minnesota Law Review 712 (2004).

[40] Valley Drug Co. v. Geneva Pharms., Inc., 344 F.3d 1294, 1309 (11th Cir. 2003).

[41] See David W. Operbeck, "Rational Antitrust Policy and Reverse Payment Settlements in Hatch-Waxman Patent Litigation," 98 Georgetown Law Journal 1303 (2010); Thomas F. Cotter, "Refining the 'Presumptive Illegality' Approach to Settlements of Patent Disputes Involving Reverse Payments: A Commentary on Honvekamp, Janis and Lemley," 87 Minnesota Law Review 1789 (2003).

[42] P.L. 108-173, 117 Stat. 2066.

[43] Ibid., §1112(a)(1).

[44] Section 505(j)(5)(B)(iv) of the Federal Food, Drug, and Cosmetic Act provides for a 180-day period of "generic exclusivity" to the first ANDA applicant in certain situations.

[45] MMA §1112(a)(1).

[46] Ibid. §1112(a)(2).

[47] Ibid. §1112(c)(1).

[48] Ibid. §1115.

[49] See, e.g, Christopher O. Estwick, "Reverse Payment Settlements: How Actavis Activated the Rule of Reason," 39 Journal of Corporate Law 859 (2014); Susan Schipper, "Bed Medicine: FTC v. Actavis, Inc. and the Missed Opportunity to Resolve the Pay-for-Delay Problem," 73 Maryland Law Review. 1240 (2014); Zhenghui Wang, "Reanalyzing Reverse-Payment Settlements: A Solution to the Patentee's Dilemma," 99 Cornell Law Review 1227 (2014).

[50] See, e.g, In re K-Dur Antitrust Litigation, 686 F.3d 197 (3d Cir. 2012); Arkansas Carpenters Health and Welfare Fund v. Bayer AG, 604 F.3d 98, 94 USPQ2d 1908 (2d Cir. 2010); In re Ciprofloxacin Hydrochloride Antitrust Litigation, 544 F.3d 1323, 88 USPQ2d 1801 (Fed. Cir. 2008); Schering-Plough Corp. v. FTC, 402 F.3d 1056, 74 USPQ2d 1001 (11th Cir. 2005); In re Cardizem CD Antitrust Litigation, 332 F.3d 896 (6th Cir. 2003).

[51] 133 S. Ct. 2223 (2013). 52Ibid. at 2237. 53Ibid.

[54] See Aaron Edlin et al., "The Actavis Inference: Theory and Practice," 67 Rutgers University Law Review. 585 (2015); Audra J. Passinault, "A Prescription for the Future: Reverse-Payment Settlements in the Wake of FTC v. Actavis Pharmaceuticals," 29 Notre Dame Journal of Law, Ethics and Public Policy 549 (2015); Allison A. Schmitt, "Competition Ahead? The Legal Landscape for Reverse Payment Settlements After Federal Trade Commission v. Actavis, Inc.," 29 Berkeley Technology Law Journal 493 (2014).

[55] 133 S. Ct. at 2229.

[56] 15 U.S.C. §45.

[57] 133 S. Ct. at 2229–30.

[58] In re Androgel Antitrust Litig., 687 F. Supp. 2d 1371 (N.D. Ga. 2010).

[59] FTC v. Watson Pharm., Inc., 677 F.3d 1298, 1312 (11th Cir. 2012).

[60] 133 S. Ct. at 2231.

[61] Ibid.

[62] Ibid. at 2225–26.

[63]Ibid. at 2237.

[64] Ibid.

[65] Ibid.

[66] Ibid. at 2239 (Roberts, C.J., dissenting).

[67] Ibid. at 2247 (Roberts, C.J., dissenting). 68Ibid. at 2238 (Roberts, C.J., dissenting). 69Ibid. at 2247 (Roberts, C.J., dissenting).

[70] See, e.g., Joshua P. Davis and Ryan J. McEwan, "Deactivating Actavis: The Clash Between the Supreme Court and (Some) Lower Courts," 67 Rutgers University Law Review 557 (2015).

[71] See Michael A. Carrier, "How Not to Apply Actavis," 109 Northwestern University Law Review Online 113 (2014).

[72] 2015 WL 3967112 (3d Cir. June 26, 2015).

[73] See Michael Carrier, "Eight Reasons Why 'No-Authorized-Generic' Promises Constitute Payment," 67 Rutgers University Law Review 697 (2015); Michael A. Carrier, "Payment After Actavis," 100 Iowa Law Review. 7 (2014).

[74] See In re Loestrin 24 FE Antitrust Litigation, 45 F.Supp.3d 180 (D.R.I. 2015); In re Lamictal Direct Purchaser Antitrust Litigation, 18 F. Supp.3d 560 (D.N.J.), vacated and remanded sub nom. King Drug Co. of Florence, Inc. v. Smithkline Beecham Corp., 2015 WL 3967112 (3d Cir. June 26, 2015).

[75] 2015 WL 3967112 (3d Cir. June 26, 2015).

[76] Ibid. at *11.

[77] Ibid. at *12.

[78] Ibid. at *14.

[79] See Benjamin M. Miller, "Antitrust Analysis After Actavis: Applying the Rule of Reason to Reverse Payments," 15 Wake Forest Journal of Business and Intellectual Property Law 382 (2015).

[80] 133 S.Ct. at 2237, 106 USPQ2d at 1964.

[81] In re Lamictal Direct Purchaser Antitrust Litigation, 18 F. Supp.3d 560 (D.N.J.), vacated and remanded sub nom. King Drug Co. of Florence, Inc. v. Smithkline Beecham Corp., 2015 WL 3967112 (3d Cir. June 26, 2015). See also In re Loestrin 24 FE Antitrust Litigation, 45 F.Supp.3d 180 (D.R.I. 2015).

[82] 2015 WL 3967112 (3d Cir. June 26, 2015).

[83] See Vikram Iyengar, "Mylan v. Warner Chilcott: A Study in Pharmaceutical Product Hopping," 19 Marquette Intellectual Property Law Review 245 (2015); Michael A. Carrier, "A Real-World Analysis of Pharmaceutical Settlements: The Missing Dimension of Product Hopping," 62 Florida Law Review 1009 (2010); Mark Metzke, "Targeting Enantiomer Product Hopping with a New 'Obviousness' Standard," 14 UCLA Journal of Law and Technology 1 (2010); Jessie Cheng, "An Antitrust Analysis of Product Hopping in the Pharmaceutical Industry," 108 Columbia Law Review 1471 (2008). See also Michelle L. Ethier, "Permissible Product Hopping: Why a Per Se Legal Rule Barring Antitrust Liability Is Necessary to Protect Future Innovation in the Pharmaceutical Industry," 3 Akron Intellectual Property Journal 323 (2009).

[84] See Lars Noah, "Product Hopping 2.0: Getting the FDA to Yank Your Original License Beats Stacking Patents," 19 Marquette Intellectual Property Law Review 161 (2015).

[85] 21 C.F.R. §314.122(a).

[86] See Jaymes V. Fairfax-Colombo and David DeMatteo, "Are Bioequivalents Really Equal? Generic Substitution in the Context of Mental Illness," 12 Indiana Health Law Review 281 (2015).

[87] See Noah, supra.

[88] See M. Sean Royall et al., Antitrust Scrutiny of Pharmaceutical "Product Hopping," 28 Antitrust 71 (Fall 2013).

[89] 787 F.3d 638 (2d Cir. 2015).

[90] Ibid. at 648.

[91] Ibid. at 649.

[92] Ibid. at 652.

[93] Ibid. at 654-56.

[94] Ibid. at 658.

[95] Ibid. at 659.

[96] S. 131 at §2.

[97] Ibid. at §3(a).

[98] Ibid. at §3(b).

[99] S. 214 at §3.

INDEX

D

E

F

G

H